T0160827

*By buying this book you are directly supporting
the mission of Green Card Voices.*

"The youth of Green Card Voices are ready to be the new leaders of our community, and their stories can inspire all of us. As immigrants, it is important that we tell our own stories—positive stories. When most representations in the media focus on war, famine, or the disasters that have harmed our home countries, it is crucial that we speak up and show the true stories of who we really are, as well as demonstrate our hopes and dreams to contribute to our communities in America. Our youth are growing up knowing that they have a home in two different places, but they already have big dreams to create a positive future. These stories will inspire other youths to use their history and their stories to teach others and help build a loving, peaceful community."
   —Osman M. Ali, Founder & Executive Director, Somali Museum of Minnesota

"*Green Card Youth Voices* exposes the stories that are often invisible. As a society, we say children are our priority . . . but do we ever listen to what they have to say? This book's power lies in ushering the truths about our immigrant children's journeys into the United States; it provides a space for our immigrant children to tell their stories in their own words. We need more spaces like *Green Card Youth Voices* right now—in hope that these stories will open up the hearts of those who don't know and validate the truths of others who actually know what it feels like to be an immigrant in the United States. Go read it."
   —Eliza Rasheed, Artist-Activist, Theater Teacher, Linwood Monroe Arts Plus

"Most of us are familiar with the stories of immigrants and refugees in general. But *Green Card Youth Voices* captures and provides even deeper insight into these young men and women who have experienced a lot of difficulties in their lives. The tearful journeys that these youths have experienced deserve to be heard. Please read it and then share it."
   —Eh Tah Khu, Co–Executive Director, Karen Organization of Minnesota

"*Green Card Youth Voices: Immigration Stories from a St. Paul High School* is a timely gift. This anthology reminds us that migration narratives of overcoming obstacles against all odds aren't only historical artifacts; they live and breathe in our communities. To the authors of this book: Thank you for sharing your stories and your dreams. We are listening."
   —Michelle Benegas, Assistant Professor, Second Language Teaching and Learning, Hamline University

"At any moment in our history, the voices of these students would be touching and powerful. At this particular moment, they are essential, as we seek to remember the importance of inclusiveness and the positive effects of diversity on our society. I dare you to read this and not be moved."
—Brian Rosenberg, President, Macalester College

"These stories inform and challenge and call to us. The hopes expressed here, the obstacles overcome, and the hard work it took these young men and women to get here challenge us to make reality the USA they have imagined. The story of each person is compelling, but this collection goes beyond that—taken all in all, they call us to the ongoing work of creating a truly inclusive, equitable, fair society and culture. You will be moved. And, I hope, moved to action."
—David O'Fallon, President and CEO, Minnesota Humanities Center

"As an immigrant to this country, I'm happy that someone is documenting immigrant stories regardless of their ethnic or national origin, as immigrants should be considered 'ambassadors of wealth' to their adopted communities. *Green Card Youth Voices* is a collection of stories that are candid, heartfelt, and honest, and they truly span the globe in their perspectives. No matter our background, we all can benefit from learning from these young people and reminding ourselves that every person has a journey, every person has a story, and every person deserves respect."
—Ramón León, Founder, President and CEO,
Latino Economic Development Center

"Resilience and hope suffuse these narratives of young immigrants as they describe their pathways to America and goals for the future. Their stories instruct and inspire, personalizing immigration issues in poignant and unforgettable ways."
—Dr. Rebecca Hawthorne, Director, Master of Arts in Organizational
Leadership Program, St. Catherine University

"To be able to share with the world what I am fortunate enough to experience every day in my classroom is a blessing. These students have individual narratives that have transformed my life and the lives of the people they have met. In our current political climate, we need to look to our youth and their voices. Every one of our children and youth deserves to be acknowledged, validated, and celebrated for the individual cultures they bring into our classrooms and society. This book is a testament to the beauty and heroism of thirty young leaders who are ready to make their mark on this world."
—Dr. Amy Hewett-Olatunde, EL Teacher LEAP High School,
2015–16 Minnesota Teacher of the Year

"Currently, America is struggling with making sense of its growing immigrant diversity in a time when the global migration of people is larger now more than any other time in history. This collection of stories—beautiful and raw and authentic—of the lives of Americans who arise from that diaspora of humanity is needed for us to arrive at a place where we can fulfill the promise of our democracy and be a nation where our differences are seen as the substance of our collective strength."

—Carlos Mariani, MN House of Representative and Executive Director, Minnesota Minority Education Partnership

"There is power in owning your own words and telling your own stories. As these honest, vulnerable, and courageous essays prove, each of our voices and our journeys are varied, each one unique and complicated, but also resilient and hopeful. Reading these essays, I am reminded of my own refugee history and how stories written and told by people like me did not abundantly exist in the 1980–90s. I feel so fortunate today that immigrant and refugee experiences are amplified by organizations like Green Card Voices. These stories are important. Urgent. "

—Saymoukda Duangphouxay Vongsay, Founder/Director of Refugenius Lab, Poet, Playwright, and Author of *Kung Fu Zombies vs. Cannibals*

"Green Card Voices is what we need now. This is our future. This book should be required reading for the entire country."

—Chad Kampe, Executive Director, Mid-Continent Oceanographic Institute

"Beautiful. Empowering young people to share their stories and giving the rest of us an opportunity to learn from them is what we need right now. My students and I are fortunate to have *Green Card Youth Voices* to help us build a more complete—and human—understanding of our world."

—Scott Glew, Social Studies Teacher, Salk Middle School, Elk River, MN

"The grace and courage of these young writers radiate from the page. *Green Card Youth Voices* is required reading for anyone with a stake in the conversation around global immigration. In other words, all of us."

—Anitra Budd, Editor and Writer, Visiting Assistant Professor of English, Macalester College

"This book helps to close the gap between the perceptions of who we are as Minnesotans and the realities. These young perspectives of those who have crossed borders are needed now more than ever, reminding us that history is now." **—Wing Young Huie, Photographer, Third Street Gallery and 2018 McKnight Distinguished Artist**

"Almost thirty-eight years ago, my parents made a tremendous sacrifice so I could be the first in the family to come to the United States and be the first to receive a college education. The voices of these students reminded me of my own immigrant journey, particularly the mixed emotions that came with the promise of the 'American Dream' while often feeling homesick for the family and friends who were left behind. Thank you Green Card Voices for engaging our immigrant youth to own and share their inspiring stories of love and courage."

—Rose Wan-Mui Chu, PhD., Professor of Urban Ed., Metropolitan State University

"*Green Card Youth Voices: Immigration Stories from a St. Paul High School* shines a light on the tremendous sacrifices and struggles faced by immigrants seeking a better life in the United States of America. This book is an effective and powerful tool for cultivating empathy and recognizing the diversity of experiences in our own community. As an immigrant and an educator, reading these stories made my heart break and then sing. I am moved by the authors' resilience, desire to feel a sense of home, and determination to make the world a better place. In giving these students a voice and platform to share their important, beautiful stories, Green Card Voices is providing hope and optimism to all of us, right when we need it the most."

—Regina Santiago, Teacher, St. Paul Academy and Summit School

"From my first reading of earlier stories, I continue to be impressed by the struggles, the dreams, the aspirations, and the achievements of these young immigrant women and men. Their stories bring alive the challenges they have faced and continue to face as they endeavor to adjust to and succeed in their new country. Despite these challenges, there is a strong sense of hope and gladness that permeates their stories. Kudos to Green Card Voices for providing a forum for voices that are rarely heard and that provide readers the opportunity to develop an appreciation of just who these new immigrants are. This is a must-read for everyone in these problematic times."

—Andrea DeCapua, EdD, Educational Consultant, MALP® LLC

"Green Card Voices is an incredible organization to have in our community. With the launch of their enlightening new book, *Green Card Youth Voices: Immigration Stories from a St. Paul High School*, they are providing a much-needed opportunity for expanded audiences to experience the stories of New Americans. It is a must-read."

—Justin Madel, Director, Festival of Nations

"In today's political climate, this book is a powerful reminder of what the United States has always represented: a refuge for people who have been persecuted and marginalized in other countries. *Green Card Youth Voices* humanizes the immigrant and refugee experiences. It is especially powerful to hear first-generation immigrants and refugees telling their own stories in their own words. I was struck by how the youth featured in the book never question their loyalties. Even as they fight for a better life in the US amidst adversities, they have hopes to better the lives of those they left behind in other countries."

—May Lee-Yang, Hmong American Refugee and Artist, Author of
Confessions of a Lazy Hmong Woman

"*Green Card Youth Voices: Immigration Stories from a St. Paul High School* is a valuable tool for educators who are serious about integrating culturally responsive practices into their daily instruction. This collection of personal essays establishes a powerful connection between the lives of young immigrants and the content that is taught in our schools. As our classrooms become increasingly filled with students from a range of backgrounds, our teaching must also begin to reflect this change. The essays and the included study guide allow teachers to capitalize on the multiple viewpoints and cultural strengths of their students. They address issues and concerns that actively engage today's students in the learning process. This authentic pedagogical resource promotes more equitable teaching practices in the classroom."

—Dr. Barbara Pierre-Louis, Cultural Activist,
Black Diaspora Studies and Language Instructor

"Like previous Green Card Voices editions, this book is an essential read for educators and others who would understand what brought young immigrants to the US, what they do, and what they will contribute to our society. But, like previous editions, it is more. When you read that a high school student feels blessed and lucky to have grown up in a refugee camp, as you will in this book, you know that you are in touch with a realm that few of us will ever reach—a realm of true wisdom born of terrible suffering, of amazing hope born of devastating loss. The stories in this book bear witness to what is worst, and best, in our world—the worst hand that fate can deal a person by sheer accident of the time and location of one's birth and the best a person can do with a life, the courage, the commitment, the refusal to give up or give in to bitterness. Here are lessons, for all who are bored, sated, dissatisfied even in abundance, and models, for all who seek to live bravely and well."

—Dr. Jill A. Watson, Assistant Professor of ESL Education, St. Olaf College;
Special Consultant on Students with Limited or Interrupted Formal Education,
Minnesota Department of Education

Green Card Youth Voices

Immigration Stories from a St. Paul High School

Lah Lah, Ahmed Hamza (C.R.) Mahamed, Anta Thosaengsiri, Nathanael Valera, Day Nya Moo, Aye Aye Win, Nima Ahmed, Isaac Flores, Jae Nay Htoo, Ah Bay Yan, Tatiana Anariba Osorio, Sha Lay Paw, Yomiyu Gafesu, Christ Taw, Say Hay Taw, Cristina Vasquez, Huoy Lin Mao, Eh Sa Kaw, Aisha Abdullahi, Oh Kler, Hla Yu Htoo, Iya Xiong, Nelly Beltran-Espitia, Wah Soe, Pare Meh, Abshir Mohamed, Kzee Ya, Javier Arreola Martell, Ma Ka Lah, Lu Lue

Authors

Tea Rozman Clark and Rachel Mueller
Editors

ISBN 13: 978-1-949523-04-1
eISBN 13: 978-1-949523-06-5
LCCN: 2017906426

Printed in the United States of America
First Printing: 2017   Second Printing: 2019
20   19   18   17   16   5   4   3   2   1

Edited by Tea Rozman Clark and Rachel Mueller

Cover design by Elena Dodevska
Interior design by José Guzmán and Shiney Her
Photography, videography by Media Active: Youth Produced Media

Green Card Voices
info@greencardvoices.org
www.greencardvoices.org

Consortium Book Sales & Distribution
34 Thirteenth Avenue NE, Suite 101
Minneapolis, MN 55413-1007
www.cbsd.com

To the authors of this book, we dedicate these pages to you in the hopes that you continue to express your authentic selves and that you find an environment that supports you. Remember, you are your story, and by sharing it you are enabling others to see themselves in your story. It is not our differences that divide us, but our judgments.

Table of Contents

Foreword

Wfled the country I was born in just as the regime we were fleeing from rolled their tanks into Saigon, shelling the airport night and day in an attempt to kill escaping families like mine. I am too young to remember, but from the multiple accounts from my other family members, it is not an exaggeration to say it was a miracle we survived.

Close to four decades later, I and some members of my family sat in a restaurant in Saint Paul. Like many refugees my age, my comprehension skills are very sharp, but my speaking skills are poor. I remember fiddling with my food and hoping no one would ask me any questions that would require too much of a response, thereby exposing my terrible Vietnamese speaking skills. The conversation turned to reminiscing about those chaotic, terrifying days we fled. Who was where, who ran and when, and who didn't make it. It struck me then, looking at my family members—just regular human beings—could walk outside, and have to weather any discrimination and ignorance brought to bear on them, when each of them has such an incredible story of survival and resistance.

Which is why the brave voices in this collection are so important.

The United States of America is a confusing place. The indigenous people of this country have to fight for something as simple as clean water, and some are considered "illegal" immigrants. There is xenophobia against those seen as "the enemy," even if our relatives fought on the same side as Americans. There is police brutality and other forms of state-sanctioned violence against Black and Brown bodies, justified by racist logics that have been present since the creation of this nation but which many believe we have moved long past.

Many of us, who have a certain color of skin or speak English a certain way or pray to someone in particular or any combination therein, are told to go back to where we come from, slander carrying an imbedded judgement: here is better than there, and you don't belong here. Which is a puzzling slur since the only people from "here" are American Indian people who do not benefit from these vicious bigoted nationalisms disguised as patriotism. Such ignorance only makes sense in a system of institutionalized oppression that centers one story and one identity as its center. But before we

i

dismiss this as harmless misunderstanding, recognize that these dangerous narratives of who is a "citizen" and who is a "foreigner" are imbedded with power and privilege, and those of us on the bottom of the binary can find our loved ones discriminated against, silenced, and deported.

There are many strategies to make our country, and our world, a better place, and one of those is telling our stories. In this collection, these gracious writers lay it all out on the table. What they had to do to come here. The waiting, the running, the hiding, the paperwork. The long hours and low-paying jobs, the English classes, the intrafamilial conflict. The storytellers here have so much to tell you, and you will come to realize that their journey is not necessarily about a point on a map. You will be in no danger of romanticizing immigrants and refugees after reading this book—they, like any other family, struggle with relationships, assimilation, poverty, and any and all other difficulties that being a human being comes with.

But they also need listeners, and readers. And here's where you do your part. Read these lovely, harrowing, funny, sad stories. Never forget the courage it takes for these writers to share their lives with you. Don't pity them—that's not what they are asking. Be proud of them, learn from them, see through their eyes, see yourselves in them. You and the world will be better for it.

Bao Phi
Program Director at The Loft Literary Center, Community Activist, Spoken Word Artist, and Author of *Thousand Star Hotel, Sông I Sing,* and *A Different Pond.*

Acknowledgments

The most important people in this project are the thirty student authors who so courageously shared their worlds. From hours of preparation in the classroom to sharing their stories on camera, from posing for portraits in the cold Minnesota winter to working with volunteers to polish their essays, these young people have put in tremendous effort to bring you these essays and video narratives. They are the heart and soul of this work. Thank you!

Several other people have been critical parts of the entire process. Dr. Amy Hewett-Olatunde, MN Teacher of the Year 2015–16 and EL teacher at LEAP High School, partnered with Green Card Voices to record and share the stories of her students. She worked with them long before they visited us at our studio, practicing the six open-ended questions we ask and making sure they understood the project, ensuring that the recording was a great success. She has been tireless in her advocacy for the students and has been foundational to bringing these essays to life.

One of the critical partnerships Dr. Hewett-Olatunde provided was a connection to Dr. Michelle Benegas, assistant professor of Second Language Teaching and Learning at Hamline University. Michelle helped organize ten Hamline master in ESL students to work one-on-one with the LEAP student authors to help them compose their personal essays. Thank you to Maddie Hillier, Natalia Petkovich, Olivia Meyer, Ellen M. Perrault, Kimberly Skramstad, Heidi Swanson, Renee Zheng, Hilary Dunn, Brigitta S. Bognar Cronin, and Patsy L. Lee for their help with this.

We contracted with Intermedia Arts' Media Active to do the video recordings and portraits. We especially want to thank Ahxuen Ybarra, DeAundre Dent, Carmela Simone, Amir Davis, Sarah Maude Griffin, and McKenna Reedquist, who did the videography and photography, and Michael Hay for supervision.

Special thanks to our foreword author, Bao Phi, who prefaced these young people's stories with reflections of his own. As an immigrant and writer himself, Bao was an excellent choice to give these stories truly meaningful perspective.

Thanks also to Principal Rose Santos of LEAP High School, who supported the project from the very beginning. Her leadership has helped make the book a success. To Josh Verges of the Pioneer Press and to Doualy Xaykaothao of MPR for seeing the value in these students' words and creating media, thank you for helping us spread the word.

Thanks to the Green Card Voices' board and staff for overseeing the project. Thank you to Executive Director, Tea Rozman Clark, who guided the project and provided the necessary leadership for this book to realize its fullest potential. Her guidance and commitment to the vision of Green Card Voices continues to motivate everyone she meets. Thank you to Jose Guzman, Green Card Voices' Graphic Designer and Video Editor, for compellingly presenting these stories and for all his work making moving video narratives. Thank you to Rachel Mueller, GCV's Program Associate, who coordinated our efforts, assisted in keeping the team on track, and made this project a success. A tremendous thank you goes to Dara Beevas-Moore and our copy editor Patrick Maloney at Wise Ink Creative Publishing for their advice, support, and encouragement. Our collaboration as well as their donations of time and consultation through the InkPossible program greatly enhanced the final product.

Thanks to our funders at the Minnesota Philanthropy Partners with the Saint Paul Foundation and the F. R. Bigelow Foundation: Dr. Eric Jolly, Sharon DeMark, Miguel Ramos, and Bruce Thao. Thanks also to the Education Minnesota Foundation's Dayonna L. Knutson. Your support of our work is what makes the wheels turn!

A huge thank you to the president and CEO of the Amherst H. Wilder Foundation, MayKao Hang, and Kristine Martin, vice president of Wilder Center Communities, for donating the venue for our book launch celebration. Upon publication of the book, the students will be able to celebrate their publishing achievements and be publically recognized because of this donation.

Thank you to Veronica Quillien, who designed the study guide and who is also the lead author of *Voices of Immigrant Storytellers: Teaching Guide for Middle and High Schools*. She is a first-generation immigrant and a PhD student in the Curriculum & Instruction Department at the University of Minnesota. We thank her for her expertise.

To all of our board members, present (Jessica Cordova Kramer, Johan Eriksson, Faraaz Mohammed, Katie Murphy-Olsen, Masami Suga, George C. Maxwell, Hibo Abdi, Tara Kennedy, Veronica Quillien, Dana Boyle, and Matt Kim) and past (Miguel Ramos, Jane Graupman, Ali Alizadeh, Laura Danielson, Jeff Corn, Ruhel Islam, Angela Eifert, and Kathy Seipp) and all others who have helped our mission along the way: thank you.

Introduction

Immigration is a central part of the American experience, and it has been a topic of national dialogue with every wave of immigration since our nation's founding. Though the details change, many fundamental reasons why people migrate remain constant: we all seek lives that are free from persecution in order for ourselves and our children to flourish. We all desire to practice our faiths without fear, to be able to provide for our families, and to have access to a good education. In fact, these values are so fundamental that even young people, like those in this book, share these dreams of better futures.

As time passes and the makeup of our population shifts, we experience cycles of change that constantly recreate the American landscape as the new immigrants assimilate into our local cultures and remind us of old debates. Woven into this "minority" narrative, but often overlooked, are the Native Americans whose land we now inhabit and the descendants of the Africans who were forcibly brought here.

The newest wave of immigration has reignited the national debate, with immigrants hailing from Latin America, Asia, and Africa, unlike previous waves where immigrants predominantly migrated from Europe. These immigrants are transforming our nation's communities by vastly increasing the percentage of diverse minorities. More than ever before, the population of the United States is made up of people from every country around the world. According to the US Census (2016) an estimated 13.3 percent of our population, or 42.3 million people, were not born in the United States.

It is now, more than ever, that organizations like Green Card Voices are being called to step forward and share the richness of the experiences and contributions that immigrants bring to our nation. It is with young new Americans in particular that we can see the resilience, courage, and endless potential that our newest neighbors embody, as you will see in this book.

Green Card Voices was established in 2013 as a storytelling platform whose aim is to build bridges and create empathy between the immigrant and nonimmigrant populations. To date, we have recorded stories from over three hundred people coming from over one hundred different countries. Each story is as unique as its teller, and each offers a glimpse into the lives of our newest neighbors. Through our video recordings—all available online and free to watch—our traveling exhibits, our book publications, and our teaching guides, we hope to make the immigrant experience visible, accessible, and relatable in order to create communities of empathy where every person can thrive.

Because nearly one in six Minnesotans under nineteen have an immigrant parent (MN Compass, Wilder Research Overview, 2016 report), it is more important than ever to share the diversity of experiences of young immigrant Minnesotans. In St. Paul, the capital city of Minnesota with a population of 295,043, 18.5 percent of people are foreign-born; 16.5 percent are Asian, 15.1 percent are Black, and 9.5 percent are Latino (MN Compass 2015). These statistics give a clue into the largest population that has migrated to the area in the past twenty years—immigrants born in Asia.

In the heart of the St. Paul immigrant community is LEAP High School, an all-immigrant high school and part of the St. Paul Public Schools system. At present it serves approximately three hundred students, more than 50 percent born in Asia, most students being from Thailand, Myanmar (also known as Burma) and Laos, and speaking Thai, Burmese, Hmong, Karen, S'gaw, Karenni, Lisu, Cambodian, and Nepali. Other languages spoken at LEAP include Afan Oromo, Oromo, Amharic, Anuak, French, Kiswahili, Somali, Bantu, and Shona from Africa; Arabic and Dari from the Middle East; Spanish and Mam from Latin America; and Chinese from Asia. Its student body is 100% immigrant and ranges in ages from fourteen to twenty-one. Thirty of these students are the authors of this book.

Green Card Youth Voices: Immigration Stories from a St. Paul High School is the third in a series of books written by young immigrants. Our first title was written by students from Minneapolis, MN, and was a national award-winner for Best Multicultural Nonfiction Chapter Book in the Moonbeam Children's Book Awards and a Foreword INDIES finalist for Young Adult Nonfiction. Our second book was written by students in Fargo, ND.

The partnership for this book began in the summer of 2016 when Tea Rozman Clark, executive director of Green Card Voices, met with LEAP High School EL teacher Dr. Amy Hewett-Olatunde and principal Rose Santos to discuss a possible book project. Although geographically the "twin" to Minneapolis, St. Paul is a vastly different city with different cultures and immigrant populations. The largest immigrant groups in Minneapolis, for example, are from East Africa and Latin America (Somalia and Mexico specifically), while in St. Paul the largest immigrant groups are from Southeast

Asia: Thailand, Myanmar (also known as Burma), and Laos. This diversity is reflected in the books. The Green Card Youth Voices Minneapolis book was written by students from Wellstone International High School where 66 percent of the students come from Africa, 32 percent from Latin America, and only 1 percent from Asia. At LEAP High School in St. Paul, 55 percent of the students come from Asia, 23 percent from Latin America, and 22 percent from Africa. Because of this, the Minneapolis and St. Paul Green Card Youth Voices books are complementary to one another, sharing the stories of students who come from vastly different countries but who are only across the river from each other.

In order to combat the effects of increased polarization in our communities, we must meet each other on common ground and from there explore our differences. In these pages you will read about desires for better education; dreams to become interpreters, nurses, and engineers; and deep commitments to family. When we are able to see ourselves in the stories of another, we work towards true empathy and understanding. For example, after several executive orders were issued halting the US's refugee resettlement program, St. Paul's mayor, Chris Coleman, expressed in a community meeting that "these are critical times, and we stand firmly" with our immigrant populations.

Green Card Youth Voices: Immigration Stories from a St. Paul High School shares the dreams and desires of St. Paul's newest generation while also offering them the opportunity to shine through their experiences and embrace their identities. We hope their courage inspires you to build a nation where we all have the freedom to pursue our dreams.

How to Use this Book

At the end of each student's essay, you will find a URL link to that student's digital narrative on Green Card Voices' website. You will also see a QR code link to that story. Below are instructions for using your mobile device to scan a QR code.

1. Using your mobile device—such as a smartphone or tablet—visit the App Store for your network, such as the Apple Store or the Android Store. Search the App Store for a "QR reader." You will find multiple free apps for you to download, and any one of them will work with this book.

2. Open your new QR reader app. Once the app has opened, hover the camera on your mobile device a few inches away from the QR code you want to scan. The app will capture the image of the QR code and take you to that student's profile page on the Green Card Voices website.

3. Once your web browser opens, you'll see the digital story. Press play and watch one of our inspirational stories.

STEP 1

Download the app.

STEP 2

Scan the QR code.

STEP 3

Watch the digital story.

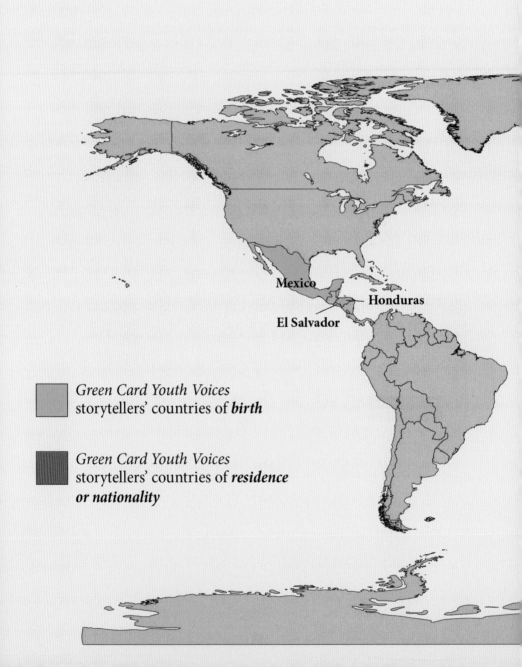

Mexico

Honduras

El Salvador

Green Card Youth Voices
storytellers' countries of *birth*

Green Card Youth Voices
storytellers' countries of *residence
or nationality*

World Map

Saudi
Arabia

Djibouti

Ethiopia

Somalia

Kenya

South Africa

Laos

Myanmar
(Burma)

Cambodia

Thailand

Personal Essays

Lah Lah

From: Tapokaw, Myanmar (Karen)
Current City: St. Paul, MN

"I HOPE MY RELATIONSHIP WITHIN MY COMMUNITY HERE KEEPS GROWING BECAUSE I WANT THEM TO KNOW MORE ABOUT MY PEOPLE, THEIR SITUATIONS, AND THE ISSUES THAT THEY ARE FACING IN THEIR LIVES NOW."

I was born in Burma and I lived there for only two years because my parents moved to the refugee camp. We moved to the refugee camp because there was a war in my village. I didn't get to spend a lot of time in the place I was born. Most of my life I spent in the refugee camp. In the refugee camp, our life was so hard. At first when we came there was no house so the refugees had to build about ten thousand houses again to live there. Before we built the houses, everybody helped each other move people and things on a big truck. Before I moved to this camp, I lived in another camp. There was a fire, so I had to move into this camp. The DKBA (Democratic Karen Buddhist Army) burned the houses at night while the refugees were sleeping. Some of the refugees got hurt, and some died.

I have two parents and one younger brother. My brother was born in the camp. I have one grandma who lives with me right now. When I moved to the camp, I didn't get to see my grandma for many years because she lived in another camp. I also had one older sister and one older brother, but they passed away while we were escaping from the Burmese soldiers. They got sick because there was a very heavy rain for about a month. My father passed away when I was in the camp. I was eleven years old, and my brother was seven years old.

When I was eight, I went to work with my father every weekend. The owner paid me depending on how much fruit I picked. My parents always prepared me to learn how to stand on my own feet, which means I don't try to depend on others and do everything that others tell me. The reason they did that is that my father had a very bad story when he was the same age as me. Both of his parents passed away when he was ten years old and his younger sister was seven years old. He had to take care of animals, and if he couldn't

1

find all the cows, he couldn't come back to the house and eat. He had to sleep in the forest. Especially, it was really hard for him because he was hungry and the rain didn't stop. Based on his experience, he didn't want me and my younger brother to live with other people when he and my mother died, because he worried that we might face the same situation.

Before the camp, my father and his friends had to work for the Burmese soldiers for many weeks, but they didn't give any food to any of them. My father and his friends had to carry supplies for the Burmese soldiers. They were walking for hours. While they walked, they would fall down because they didn't have energy to keep walking forward. They were kicked with strong boots and hit with guns by the soldiers when they stopped walking or fell. When they got home and ate food, some of them got sick because their digestive systems were not working as before.

I was the only one who wanted to come to the US. When I was ten or twelve, I talked to my parents about applying to the US, but they didn't want to come because they didn't know any English. They never went to school, so they were kind of scared to come to a new country without knowing the English language. I asked them more than three or four times but they didn't want to come. But after my father passed away, my brother was lonely, and he really wanted to come to the US. He talked to my mom about coming to the US, and they both agreed to apply. The reason my mom came to the US is that she wanted me and my brother to get an education and then go back to our country.

In 2012, my family applied to come to the US. It took us about one year to get a chance to come. I didn't think we would get to Saint Paul because my grandma refused to come to the US over and over again. She had dementia and she forgot easily. Every time we told her that we wanted to go to America, she didn't want to go because she didn't want to leave her country. My grandma and my mother lived apart when we were in the refugee camp, but if we came here, there wouldn't be anyone to take care her. For that reason, she had to come with us, but she didn't want to come. She wanted to stay there, but she couldn't live by herself because she is old.

When I came, I wasn't prepared because I didn't think that I could make it to the US. I went to school every day, and on Friday, I came to the US. I didn't pack up my things or clothes because I saw some people were sent back when they were refused or had health problems. When we almost got to the airport, my grandma refused to come, and they almost sent us back to the refugee camp.

I didn't get a chance to sleep on the airplane because there were some Karen refugees who came from the same camp as me, and they didn't speak any English. On the airplane, they didn't know how to use the toilet and they were scared that they would get stuck in the bathroom. They woke me up so many times, but I was happy that I helped them. We were separated on the last airplane because we went to different states. When I got here, I was thinking that the place was nice and I believed that I could find happiness here. I didn't feel happy, and I got sick. I didn't like the weather or food at all. I wanted to go back to my country because there were not many people who could visit you like in the country where I grew up. In the country where I grew up, everybody visits everyone almost every night. Here, it is not easy to visit each other unless you have a car.

In my first months here, I helped my aunt and cousins a lot. I didn't go to school right after my first week because the school ended in June. I got here in July. I helped my aunt and uncle take care of my little cousin at home, and I also helped my other cousin send them to the school bus stop and waited for them at the drop off stop to come home. It was a very good experience for me because I knew that when the next school year started, I wouldn't have a hard time finding my school bus or my school bus stop.

After two months, I went to school. I started in ninth grade in LEAP High School. I didn't speak any English in my first few months in school. I started my English at level one, which is the lowest level. I was so nervous and excited at the same time. I didn't know anyone, even though there were many Karen students, because they were from different camps. I was too shy to talk to my teachers, but they kept asking me more questions. Karen students didn't come and talk to me because they thought I was not Karen. After two or three days, they came and talked to me, and I didn't feel nervous or scared anymore. In my first year, I met my best friend in school and I started to feel that I belong to this school. I remember when we were in class, she always helped me because she lived here about one or two years. She graduated in June 2016. Now I'm in twelfth grade. I will graduate this year.

My neighborhood is getting better than before because everyone knows each other and helps each other. Before, I didn't know any of my neighbors, and most of my neighbors spoke different languages. When my mom communicates with my neighbors, she uses her sign language because they can't speak each other's languages. Now that we know each other, we are like big family. Every time I get home, one of my friends comes to my house to visit me. Now we are like brothers and sisters. We cook together and eat together. I am doing fine with my school, and I have many friends. My school is the number-one place that gives me hope and makes me believe that I can achieve my goals. I never thought I could achieve my goals in my life because I never thought that I would graduate from high school.

I always take care of my grandma on the weekend. Sometimes, I volunteer in the nursing home because I want to be a nurse. In the summertime, me and my family go to the park and have parties. Most of the time, we go with some of my relatives. We bring food, and we also fish at the lakes. We cook and eat together, and it reminds us of my country. Every time we go to park, we go to different park.

I have been involved in many activities outside and inside of school. I am a student at the 3M STEP program and also a CNA (Certified Nursing Assistant) at Saint Paul Community College. I am a student ambassador at LEAP High School, and I also joined the drama club. I love to try different things because it is exciting. I also learn from my experiences. It is very good to experience because I know which jobs fit me and which do not. In March 2017, I went to the Minnesota State Capitol to tell my story, and I was so happy to get a chance to talk about my journey coming to the US, my past experience, and my school here. That was the best thing I ever did in my life.

I hope my relationship within my community here keeps growing because I want them to know more about my people, their situations, and the issues that they are facing in their lives now. I believe that the more they know about me and my people, the more they are willing to help my people. I plan to go back and help my people the best I can. My goal is to become a nurse. When I become a nurse, I would like to go back to my country and volunteer there. I don't want to live there because I know that it is not safe for me to live there like before. My goal is to build a hospital or clinic there, and I know that I will need a lot of people to help with that. I would need a lot of people who would support me, help me, and work together with me. The reason I want to build a hospital is because I know that they really need that. I will find out what they need and report it to the people here to help me and support me. I will not live there. Before I go back, I will contact an organization that will work with me. I will volunteer there for about one to two years, then I will come back to the US.

One thing that I can never forget about is my mom's experience in this city. It was so hard for my mom to get transportation here. Every time we asked for help with the transportation, neighbors were so angry and looked down on us. Before they helped us, they said so many hurtful words to us. Sometimes, I cried because of that, but I always tried to be strong. I was so angry at those people. This year, I got a car and my mom didn't have to call anybody. Sometimes people called my mom and asked for help and I helped them the best I could. My parents always tell me to help others the best I can. I am so angry when I think of what those people have done to my mom. The more I think about that, the more I get angry, but I know that it is not good to keep seeing others' mistakes.

VIDEO LINKS

greencardvoices.org/speakers/lah-lah

Jeddah,
Saudi Arabia

Ahmed Hamza (C.R.) Mahamed

From: Jeddah, Saudi Arabia (Somali)
Current City: St. Paul, MN

> "IT'S ALL ABOUT LOVING EACH OTHER AND COMMUNICATION WITH OTHER PEOPLE. PEOPLE THINK OF IMMIGRANTS AS PEOPLE WHO COME FROM OTHER COUNTRIES WHO ARE BAD. MINNESOTA IS FULL OF IMMIGRANTS."

My name is Ahmed Hamza Mahamed, and I am Somali. Well, my parents are from Somalia, and I was born in Jeddah, Saudi Arabia on August 20, 1997. I was four years old when my parents decided to move to South Africa. Before, I was in Somalia for two months, but I was young at the time. I think I was like three years old, so my mom was carrying me, so I don't know what it was like.

My parents first stayed in Somalia for few months, and then we went to South Africa in 2000. We moved to Port Elizabeth, South Africa, and we stayed there for fifteen years. My mom then got engaged to my stepdad. He had five kids. My mom was working at a restaurant. Life in South Africa was better than in Saudi Arabia because in Saudi Arabia most people, like my mom and dad, were denied rights. They could not get papers, so they were in hiding, and if they were caught they would get sent back to Somalia.

In South Africa I attended school, a primary school called Nasrudin. I started learning English, and not only English but Afrikaans also. I also attended high school, Uitenhage High School, until grade eleven.

People think I'm the kind of person that people get along with, I'm kind, and I don't like people who are rude. I'm not rude.

My hobby was soccer, and I used to play for different clubs. I also played for the school. I played for Somali organizations in South Africa, which were called OSU. They do kind of okay. In South Africa, I remember I used to go to straight from the mosque to the field.

I think I was fourteen years old, and there was a team called Somali United, and I wanted to play, but according to my age they said I was too young. So, I waited until I was fifteen. When I was fifteen years old, it was the first time they let me play. I was playing defender, right back, and it was going good, so they decided for me to play every game. I remember before coming to the USA there was a cup, and I played and we won the cup.

Another organization I used to play with was called Swift Response. It was a nongovernment organization, which I could've played for two years or three years and I could have traveled around the world. There was another tournament Swift Response organized, like a league. We won and I got best player for the tournament and got put on the cover page of the newspaper.

I used to play chess in high school. We weren't good, but we played for fun and to learn from our mistakes.

The only happy times I had in South Africa were playing soccer in clubs and with friends. The other times, I was scared when I was walking in the streets.

In South Africa, most Somalis were being attacked by xenophobia, and most of the shops were burned, most of them got killed, some woman got raped, one which was our neighbor. She was a pregnant lady; she was nine months pregnant, and she was at home while her husband was at work. Three men came and raped her and took most of her stuff. The next morning my mom went there and saw the door was open. She saw that the lady was killed. They hung her. The Somali community came together and they found the men, and they were put in jail for life.

When I was twelve, a group of teenagers threw stones in my eyes, which made me bleed. It caused me a lot of problems. I had an operation because of this. The doctor said I had cataracts.

Most of the Somalis joined a UN organization, and they help them to the US now. The government made the process faster because they saw the Somali people were being tortured by the South Africans because they thought they were taking their jobs. But they were opening shops. That's why my parents joined the organization in 2009.

In 2016, I think it was August 12, I came from school and my parents told me that we were ready for the flight, and that was exciting. My friends told me they were going to miss me. People told me that the US was great place to be. I had mixed feelings because I would miss my friends, but I was excited for a new life. I kind of miss them all and they miss me too.

We went to the airport in Johannesburg. It's called O. R. Tambo International Airport. And from there we flew to New York and from New York to Chicago and from Chicago to Minnesota. It was exciting, and it was fun. I came August 20; that's on my birthday. I think that was the best gift.

When I arrived, I was scared. How would I meet new people? New friends? But everyone was so nice to me. I can say it's better than South Africa. People are respectful, nonviolent, and far better. My stepdad's family, my uncles, were here, so they picked us from the airport and brought us to the new house. Minnesota was different. It was quiet. In South Africa, the neighborhood was noisy. The first three days it felt so boring. I only stayed at home. After months and months, I got to meet new people. I met them in school.

The caseworker told me I should start by the ninth grade, but in South Africa I was in the eleventh grade, I was supposed to be in the twelfth grade now. When they told me I should start the ninth grade, I was unhappy because I already finished that grade a long time ago. So I said no. My small brother went to school with my other brothers and my sisters, and I stayed at home for like one month. Then I got someone's number—I think it was the school's soccer coach—and I phoned him, and he told me to come to the school. I told my parents about that, so we took the taxi and we went to the school.

I signed up for the school. It's called PSA, and I attended it for two months. It was kind of fun, but I lived in Saint Paul and the school is in Minneapolis, and I had to wake up at five o'clock in the morning. I told the case manager that was working with us that it was too far, and she told me that there's a school for immigrants called LEAP High School and that I would like it. So she signed me up for that school.

I love this school. It's better. At LEAP High School, they told me it's not about the grade; it's about the level you're in, like 1A to 4A. So now I attend 3B. Next semester, I will be like 3A or 4B, so I have like two more levels left for me. I am excited to graduate. This school gave me the opportunity. It is a school of immigrants, so I feel like I belong. I think this is a great school for all people new to America. I am the same as the other students. They all came from all around the world.

After school, I just go home and I just eat. Sometimes my friends pick me up and we go to Como Park and play soccer. I love soccer. I'm living with my stepdad and my mom and my seven brothers and sisters. My big brother is twenty years old, just one year older than me, and my other one is sixteen. I have three sisters and four brothers. The youngest one is five or six years old. Before my father got engaged to my mom he was engaged to another woman with whom he had three kids. Two are living Saudi Arabia now. One is married and has a kid and the other is looking for job. I speak to her every day on Facebook. She asks me about how the life is in America, and I tell her it's great.

The third is living in Somalia and is disabled. She tells me that my father's living in Somalia somewhere, and things are not going well for him. I never saw him, and my big sister told me he has kidney problems. People are living in poverty, and so my sister asked me if I could work and send him money or something to try to help him. I never saw him, but he's my dad, and I will do whatever it takes to help him. I do want to see him, and he's too old now, but I really do want to see him. My sister tells me I should send a visa or something, and she really wants to come to the USA. She can't come now with President Trump's ban.

Life in the USA is way better than it was in South Africa. The thing that is worrying me the most is my dad and my other family who are not in the USA. I really would like them to be here with me.

I don't think that President Trump's ban is a good idea because people who are living in the US have friends and family who are living in Somalia. What do you think it will be like for them to communicate? What about if they want to come here because things are not going well for them? I think President Trump's going to be a false president. Who knows if my dad's going to be alive in four years; anything can happen. Like I said, he has kidney problems. I really want to see him before four years from now. I really wanted to see my sisters, but four years is a long, long time. There's no guarantee they're going to be alive for four years. I don't think what Trump is doing is right, to say they can't help people who are in need. I don't think he should ban people from coming to the USA because what they heard is that the USA is a great place where all nations live. You can't ban them from coming here. In the future I want to be independent, because I am living with my parents now. At a young age I always wanted to be a professional soccer player, but I think that I should work hard on it. I also have a second opinion, which is being a teacher. I'm going to be an English teacher or study. I'll go to college, I will study at college and maybe I will be a teacher.

It's all about loving each other and communication with other people. People think of immigrants as people who come from other countries who are bad. Minnesota is full of immigrants. President Trump doesn't want immigrants in the country, and he doesn't like immigrants. I don't think he should say that because he doesn't know where they come from and their backgrounds. We should communicate with each other and learn about each other's cultures and languages.

I also want to help those that are in need, not only me. And, for example, people who are living in Somalia. I will always do whatever I can to help them because they also need help. You can't just live in luxury on your own; you need to help others who are in need also.

VIDEO LINKS

greencardvoices.org/speakers/ahmed-hamza-c-r-mahamed

Pak Chom,
Thailand

Anta Thosaengsiri

From: Pak Chom, Thailand (Hmong)
Current City: St. Paul, MN

"I REMEMBER MEETING FAMILY MEMBERS WHO WERE LIKE STRANGERS TO ME BECAUSE I'D NEVER MET THEM BEFORE."

I am Hmong. I lived in Thailand. I speak two languages—Thai and Hmong. My life back in Thailand was complicated. We were always moving. My grandparents lived in Laos. In 1975, they moved to Thailand. The reason why they moved to Thailand was that there was a war back there. They left Laos to live in a camp.

They lived in a refugee camp called Veenay in Thailand. My parents met each other in that camp. They married and moved back to Laos because my grandparents didn't want to come to the USA. They lived there for four years, and then I was born. I have five siblings. My two older sisters were born in Thailand. I'm the middle one. I have another sister, and my brother is the youngest. We lived in Laos for eight years, and then my parents and I moved back to Thailand. We couldn't go to the city at that time because we didn't have the citizenship yet. If we went to the city and the police saw us, they would catch us and put us into the jail. So we waited until we got the citizenship, and we moved to the city. After a few years, we moved to Tog in Thailand. I went to first grade in Tog, then we moved to Phayao. However, I had to go to first grade again. In Thailand they put all the ages together in one class. No matter what age you are, you have to start at first grade and go all the way through grade twelve. When I was young, I had to move a lot. I had to repeat a grade whenever I moved to a different place.

We lived in Phayao for four years. Then we moved to a refugee camp again. We lived there for five years. Then we moved back to Khek Noi and got a visa to move to the USA. When my two older sisters were seventeen and eighteen, we applied to come together. The process took a long time and before we knew the answer my sisters were overage. We came to the United States because my parents wanted a better life and education for us. I was sad because I had to leave my two sisters over there. I know the feeling that my sisters feel right now.

On my first airplane ride, I was scared because I hadn't ridden one before, and also it was noisy. My father told me that an airplane wasn't as noisy as a car, but for me, it's noisier. When it flew up in the air, I felt dizzy. I didn't like it. It smelled bad. I only drank water. It took almost three days.

It's very different. I had imagined that the USA was a beautiful place where everything was nice, but it wasn't. My first month was difficult because I didn't know any English. I didn't understand what people were saying to me, and I was embarrassed. I remember meeting family members who were like strangers to me because I'd never met them before. At first it was hard for us to communicate because I grew up with the Thai community and I feel most comfortable speaking Thai, and they grew up American, so they spoke English.

I had to go to a new school. LEAP High School is my first school in America. My first day was so embarrassing, scary, and exciting at the same time. The way I communicated with the teacher was just yes and no. My life now is better. This my third year and I know how to communicate with teachers and friends. I can speak English now. My whole lifestyle changed, from what I eat to what I wear and what I do every day.

Something that I like to do every weekend is to make crafts with ribbons and hair things. I bend the ribbons to make flowers. I also like to take some paper and glue it together and just fold it up to make books. I write some stories and draw. When I make things like that, I feel relaxed. It calms me down.

I also joined the Girl Scouts with people from school. I also volunteer as an event coordinator in a church youth group. For youth group we do a lot of things. We do fundraisers and we make food to sell to the members in church and people outside the church. I like to cook Thai desserts.

This summer, I'm planning to go to the Hubbs Center to take classes to prepare for college. We're going camping this summer. I'm going on three camping trips: The first one will have women and men, and I will come to cook for them. The second is for the youth group from church. It's in St. Cloud. We have a lot of activities to do over there. This year we have a talent show going on for each group. My group is going to dance. The last one is for Boy and Girl Scouts.

The subject I like the most in school is CNA (Certified Nursing Assistant) class. Before I wanted to be a teacher, however, I've found I want to be a nurse. I've found in CNA class we learn some skills that we can use in our lives, how to take care of people, how to talk with people, and how to be patient with older people. For this class, I volunteer every weekend at the Episcopal Home. The language in the textbook we use in CNA is very difficult for me. It's college-level, but I try my best to do it. I believe that it is through these hardships that I will become smart and strong so I can be who I am today.

I hope to be a nurse, and I hope I graduate and go back to my country to help my community to be better. There's not a lot of healthcare over there. There are twelve villages in the city, but we only have one clinic for the whole city. They didn't have any doctors, only a few nurses. I hope to be a part of the clinic to give what I can to the community.

VIDEO LINKS

greencardvoices.org/speakers/anta-thosaengsiri

Mexico City,
Mexico

Nathanael Valera

From: Mexico City, Mexico
Current City: St. Paul, MN

"I WANTED TO SEE NEW PLACES AND TO MEET NEW PEOPLE BECAUSE I FELT THAT THERE WASN'T A PURPOSE FOR ME IN MEXICO."

My name is Nathanael. I wasn't a refugee in a camp, and I didn't pass through war. So I consider my life very privileged.

My mom and my dad came to Saint Paul when they were around eighteen years old. Then I was born here in Saint Paul. When I was one year and eight months old, my mom decided to take me back to Mexico because my dad was deported and she didn't want to be here alone. I used to ask my mom, "Why did you bring me here? I could have had a better life and more opportunities in America."

My mom left me with my grandparents while she went back with my father to a ranch. I remember that they were worried about me because I didn't want to try the food. My grandfather told me, "Eat by yourself or I will shove some food in your mouth." I refused to eat, so he grabbed a bunch of food and he stuck it in my mouth. That was the first time I liked the food that my grandmother cooked.

When I turned five, I started to see the good things about my life. My mom came back to live with us. We lived close to the church, so I went to church almost every day and I had a lot of family living around.

Kindergarten was hard for me. I didn't speak with anyone, and I sat alone. My teachers called my mom because I wasn't doing anything, but then I met a boy and we became friends. I had someone to play with, and I didn't feel alone anymore. Things started to get better because I felt that I belonged to my family and my school, but it didn't last.

There was a fight between my grandfather and his sisters, so we moved. The new house wasn't quite ready to live in, but we didn't have options. It was the first time that I remember my family living together. My mom, my sister, my uncle, my aunt, my grandfather, and my grandmother all lived together in the same house. It was quite nice because I never felt alone. I went to a new school and had the same problems again. I didn't make any friends. I was smaller than the other kids. My father turned out not to be the kind of father you would like to be around. My mom was scared that one day he would go to school and pick my sister and me up and run away with us.

After a few months, I received the news that my mom was going to have a baby. My mom and dad had a lot of discussions. My mom was scared because my brother had a syndrome. Lucky for us, we had a grandfather who would protect my mother and my little brother. He wanted my brother to be born. He said to my mom, "You have to have this baby." He thought that it was a blessing to have a baby and that there was a reason for everything.

When she had my brother, Jaziel, the doctors told her that he would not live too long. The longest that he would live was fifteen years or something like that. Now, he is thirteen years old and he is living in Mexico. He is doing well right now. He opened our mind up to see the world and its beauty. So it was a blessing, like my grandfather told us.

Another turning point in my life was when my grandfather passed away in September of 2006. We did not expect it, and we were very upset. He was an important person in my life, but the feeling grew stronger when he passed away. His presence in my life and his passing made me who I am right now. I saw him as my mentor, and I want to become wise and compassionate like he was. He was a humanitarian, putting everyone's needs first instead of his.

When that happened, I was going to middle school and I started questioning the purpose of life and why we have to die. I didn't realize until years later that it just happens. It was hard for everyone. But now I feel like I was selfish because I was just thinking about how I felt and I didn't think about how my family felt. I acted irrationally, and that brought more pain to my family. Nothing made sense anymore. I stopped paying attention in class, skipped classes, and stopped studying. I tried to run away a couple times too. A year later, my grandmother, my uncle, and my aunt decided to move to another house. Instead of moving with them, my mom and my siblings decided to stay with my dad. That time, my dad connected with us and I started to know him better, but I still felt lonely. After a while, my father decided to go his own way. We decided to move in with my grandmother, my aunt, and my uncle.

I had US citizenship because I was born in Saint Paul. I remember that my mom used to tell me all the time, "You got to be prepared, because one day, believe me or not, your uncle is gonna come for you and he's gonna take you to the United States."

When my uncle came to visit us in Mexico a few years ago, I wasn't ready to leave behind my family and my home. But I decided to come just because I wanted to experience more things. I wanted to see new places and to meet new people because I felt that there wasn't a purpose for me in Mexico. When I came to the United States, I didn't know what to do or have any plans. I was just hanging around with my uncle. It wasn't until two months into living in the United States that one of my uncles enrolled me in a school on University Avenue called the Hubbs Center, where I started to learn English. When I came, I knew no English except for "hi" and "thank you," and that was not enough most of the time.

My cousins, the ones that lived here, didn't talk to me. I didn't know what to do, so I spent six months going to the Hubbs Center, where I met lots of people. I met some old people who taught me lessons about life and the mistakes they made. They told me not to focus only on work but also to get an education.

I met a lady who was friends with my uncle, and she told me about this place called LEAP High School. I decided to enroll. I felt more comfortable knowing that the people here were young just like me and that we had similar pasts. I made lots of friends. I'm hoping to graduate this year, and I'm also working part-time.

In the future, I'd like to travel around the world and meet people and share stories. Right now, I am trying to learn how to live in the present.

VIDEO LINKS

greencardvoices.org/speakers/nathanael-valera

Mape,
Myanmar

Day Nya Moo

From: Mape, Myanmar (Karen)
Current City: St. Paul, MN

> "AT FIRST, I DIDN'T FEEL GOOD IN MINNESOTA BECAUSE I DIDN'T KNOW HOW TO SPEAK ENGLISH OR ANYTHING. I FELT LIKE I DIDN'T WANT TO LIVE HERE ANYMORE. I WANTED TO GO BACK TO MY OWN COUNTRY, BUT I COULDN'T DO ANYTHING."

I was born in Burma, in a village called Mape. When I was one year old, my parents moved to a Thai refugee camp called Mae Ra Moe. We couldn't live in the Burma village anymore because Karen and Burmese soldiers were fighting. We had to move to a safe place.

When I was five years old, my family went to the camp. My parents wanted me to go to school in the camp. I started to go to kindergarten and I continued to study until sixth grade because I wanted to learn more. I wanted to do that, too. You had to pay to go to school. Our parents felt so lucky because we got to go to school and learn so we could have better lives.

We would play many games in the camp. There was a group game where we would run around a circle. We would play a game like tag. If someone caught you, you had to say something.

We didn't have enough food in the camp. If we didn't have enough food, we would help each other by sharing the food. Some people would sneak out of the camp to find more food. My mama stayed in the house to take care of us and my father would go to another place to find a job to get money to buy food. My father would fix roofs for his job.

In 2010 or 2011, me and my brother wanted to move to the United States, but we did not know how to get here or use the application form so we could come here. So we asked our parents to apply for us, and then they said they would do it. We were so excited that they applied for us so we could come here to the United States. We all came to the United States together.

The UN sent the letter to my parents that said we could go to the United States. On June 15, we arrived in Mae Sot. In Mae Sot, we stayed while we had a health check. They said we were healthy. We took the bus to take a flight to Bangkok. We slept there one night, and in the morning we started to take the other flight to Japan. Then we arrived in Japan, and then we took the other flight to Minneapolis. Then, when we got there, our cousins were waiting for us. We got off the Minneapolis plane and then they took us to our new house in the United States. Our family was in one house together. My cousins are in a different house but they still live close to us.

At first, I didn't feel good in Minnesota because I didn't know how to speak English or anything. I felt like I didn't want to live here anymore. I wanted to go back to my own country, but I couldn't do anything. One of my first memories in Minnesota happened in the morning. My brother, my little sister, and I were so sad. We went to play in the playground, but there was an American girl and we didn't know any English. We saw her at the playground, and then I came back home to cry because we didn't know how to speak English.

We did not like the food too much when we first came to Minnesota. We still get to make some of the food from home. We will shop at Karen grocery stores and make the food. When we first were in Minnesota, we went to different stores and they had different kinds of foods. I went to the Mall of America with my Oma and Opa. I felt like it was too big. When I walked around I felt dizzy because it was so big. Sometimes we went to the Como Zoo to see the different kinds of animals. I liked seeing the monkeys with the mustaches.

When I started school, I was so happy because I found an old friend. We knew each other from our country. There was a class where they helped me because I didn't know how to do anything. The teacher also understood that we didn't know how to speak English. They talked to us in English, but in a way that we could understand. I want to learn how to speak English more. I found other Karen people at school and became friends with them. After school, I do my homework and sometimes I help my mom cook. I like cooking. I like to cook vegetables with rice.

My parents are both here, but only my father has a job. He cuts the meat. He works in a different city. My older brother's name is Nick Ku Htoo. He is twenty years old, and he works right now. My oldest sister is November Moo. She's in eleventh grade now. My younger brother is Tae Ku Htoo. He is in eighth grade. And the last one, my sister, her name is Eh Pur Soe Moo and she is in sixth grade right now. We like to hang out together.

When we have free time, my brother and my sister like to draw pictures. They always ask each other, "What should I draw?" And then my brother says, "Draw the cartoon." And then she draws. Sometime they will play games, like a zombie game. But sometimes, me and my younger sister, we watch movies. Our favorite is Korean. We like to go shopping and we do homework together when we have free time. I also like to play volleyball with my friends. We go to play in the park. I also like to go to church with my friends.

We still talk to my relatives that are in Thailand. They stayed in the camp. They want to come to America, but they are new to the camp, so they have to wait. We call them on their phone. I would like to go visit Thailand someday. My relatives are there and I miss them. I want to stay in Saint Paul. I want to stay close to my parents.

I have been here for almost six years. I am still studying in the United States at the high school. I am in twelfth grade. The subjects that I like are math, science, reading, and writing because I want to become a nurse in the future, and I want to become a teacher too, so I am trying to study in high school right now. I want to be a nurse and go back to Thailand. My people need nurses in the hospitals, and I want to help them.

VIDEO LINKS

greencardvoices.org/speakers/day-nya-moo

Tak,
Thailand

Aye Aye Win

From: Tak, Thailand (Karen and Burmese)
Current City: St. Paul, MN

> "I WAS EXCITED TO BE HERE BECAUSE I WANTED TO GO INTO THE TALL BUILDINGS. I REMEMBER WHEN A FRIEND OF MY MOM TOOK ME TO THE MALL OF AMERICA. I WAS RIDING THE ROLLER COASTER AND IT WAS SO HIGH, SO I WAS SO SCARED!"

My name is Aye Aye Win, and I was born in a refugee camp in Thailand. My parents were born in Burma, and later they moved to Thailand because of all the war, and then we were together in Thailand. My mom was a seller and my dad was a farmer. My mom sold alcohol, vegetables, and a lot of stuff. My dad grew a lot of vegetables on a farm. Sometimes we shared the vegetables with our neighbors and sometimes we sold them.

I loved living in the refugee camp because we could go into the forest or to the waterfalls. We could go out of the camp, but we needed permission. There were not a lot of people because some people were moving to America. There were more Karen than other groups of people. There were songs in Karen and Burmese, but when I was there I only listened to Karen songs. We played volleyball, jump rope, and a game with five rocks. I liked to live in the refugee camp because they gave us free food, like rice and beans, and also oil and coal. The amount of food you got depended on your family members. The food was enough for me in the camp, but sometimes we had to buy food. They gave us free food once a month, every month, but sometimes we had to buy it. The food was rice and some other things. We had to buy fish and a lot of other kinds of food. Once a month they gave free clothes too.

My parents supported me and my sister going to school. If you failed, the teacher would hit you with a stick or you would have to do a hundred squats. Sometimes you had to run in front of the school and sometimes you had to stand in front of the school. You could not use your cell phone. If the teacher caught you, they would hold onto it for the whole day. After school, I played with my friends and I went shopping.

In Thailand, you have to pay to go to school. You had to pay for each year of school. If you did not have money, you could not go to school. So

25

my parents had to support us. My mom borrowed money so we could go to school. They worked hard for us. In 2011, while I was in Bangkok, my parents got divorced. I felt sad. After the divorce, my dad moved to Burma and I lived with my mom in Thailand, but I still communicated with my dad. He still lives in Burma. I still talk to him on the phone.

My sisters and I had to leave the camp because we didn't have enough money. When my parents told me we were moving to the US, I was in Bangkok with my sister. We worked at a factory in Bangkok cutting chicken meat. My sisters and I worked there about a couple years. The factory was really big, and people from Thailand and Burma worked there. My mom called my sister and told us to come back to the refugee camp so we could go to the US. It took about a year for us to get here. My mom wanted to go to the US in 2009. She wanted us to have a better life and better education. My dad didn't want to go then, and that's why it took so long. We left in June 2014.

Before we left, an interviewer asked us questions in Thai, but there was an interpreter for us too. It was very difficult. They asked you a lot of questions. I think it took about two or three days to finish the interview.

When I was on the plane, I was scared because I didn't speak any English. I remember that I had to go to the bathroom, but I didn't know how to speak any English, so I was nervous to ask. I stayed in my seat the whole time because I didn't want to ask and it was hard to open the bathroom door. When I was thirsty and wanted a drink, I was afraid to ask. I didn't know how to ask. I wasn't sitting next to my mom or sisters, so it was more difficult. I was sitting by an American man, and I was worried he might try to speak to me in English.

I came to the US in the summer, and I felt strange. Everything's different from my country. The buildings were very tall, there were a lot of cars, and the houses, people, and food were different. There is food from my country you can buy here. There are Karen stores you can buy the food from.

A friend of my mom helped us with transportation and other things. She had a car. She had been here about seven years before us. We first had an apartment in Woodbridge and Roseville. It was clean but too expensive. My aunt bought a house and then we all moved to that house. We moved there because they already knew each other. They had a car we could use. We only lived there for four or five months and then moved to the apartment we are in now. There were too many people in the house so we left. The apartment we are living in now has all Karen people, except a few Hmong groups.

I was excited to be here because I wanted to go into the tall buildings. I remember when a friend of my mom took me to the Mall of America. I was riding the roller coaster and it was so high, so I was so scared! We also went to different places that I have never been, like Valley Fair, parks, stores, and the movie theater. Valley Fair was scarier because the roller coasters went very high! They were so exciting. When I went to the movie theater, I felt like I was an American. I ate popcorn and saw a history movie.

When I first went to school, I was nervous because I didn't have any friends and I didn't speak any English. My first school was Fairview Alternative High School. The teachers there were nice and very helpful. They supported me and helped me with speaking English. After Fairview, I came to LEAP High School. LEAP is nice too. There are a lot of Karen people, and the students are all nice and helpful. Now, I think that things are much better than before because I know how to speak English and I can help my family.

My hobbies are acting and singing; at home, my mom thinks I'm crazy, but those are my two favorite hobbies! I watch a lot of movies, too, like horror movies, drama, funny movies. I watch American movies, Chinese movies, and Japanese movies. I like to hang out with friends on the weekends. We go shopping.

I'm in grade twelve, and I'm going to graduate next year. After I graduate, I'm going to go to a college for about four or five years to become an interpreter. I'm going to help immigrants. I would want to help immigrants who are coming to America. I would also want to help in a hospital. I really would like to be a nurse too.

VIDEO LINKS

greencardvoices.org/speakers/aye-aye-win

Djibouti City,
Djibouti

Nima Ahmed

From: Djibouti City, Djibouti (Somali)
Current City: St. Paul, MN

"WHEN I WAS SIXTEEN, MY PARENTS KICKED ME OUT BECAUSE THEY FOUND OUT THAT I WAS GAY. AFTER I MOVED OUT, I LIVED IN A SHELTER FOR SEVERAL MONTHS. I FELT LONELY AND ISOLATED BECAUSE I HAVE NEVER EXPERIENCED LIFE ALONE."

My mom and dad were born in Somalia. They met in the city of Galkayo. After two months of dating, my dad asked for her hand. My grandpa gave away my mom, and that's how they got married.

My childhood was really simple. I was born and raised in a refugee camp called Ali-Addeh in Djibouti with my family. My dad was working in the city to find us our meals every day. My mom stayed with us to raise us. She would fetch water and collect wood. She would also travel to a closer village using a donkey to get our food supplies. My dad would go to the city and work. My sister also went to the city to work and try to find a job to earn money so we could go to school. The city was two hours away from the refugee camp that we were living in at the time. My dad would sometimes take the city bus and the train to go there because nobody had cars. We couldn't afford it. My oldest brother went to school, but I never had the chance to go. I wanted to take care of my sisters and help my mom to raise the kids. Even though I was only six years old, my mother taught me how to cook and clean and do everything. I was the only one who was there to help. The others were all married and didn't stay with us because they thought it was too hard to stay at the refugee camp.

One day, I was out playing with my younger brother. A leader from the camp came to me and asked for my name, and I told her. She said, "Your family's name is on the board." The board was the place where people had their names on when they were going to America. I couldn't believe it. I ran back to my house, and I said to my mom, "I think we're going to America." My mom couldn't believe me. She called my dad, and she told him that we were going to America. My dad also couldn't believe it. He came to the camp and asked the leaders, and they told him, "You have an interview." When we went to the interview, everything was perfect. They told us, "Get ready, and you'll be in America in two years."

My dad started to work in a garage that my brother-in-law owned. He had to save money for us to get ready for the process. My mom was doing the same. While we were waiting for the immigration process, my oldest brother graduated from high school. My brother went to the city to help out my dad. We bought a lot of traditional clothes and tried to be as ready as possible.

The day before we flew to America, a lot of my friends and relatives came together, and we had a big party. Everyone was crying and saying, "When you go to America, don't forget us. You're our best friend." My grandma cried a lot because she couldn't go with us. She went to the airport with us and she stayed with us the whole time until we had to fly. People gave us a lot of money and bought us clothes and coats because when we were living in the refugee camp, my dad couldn't afford anything.

When I got on the plane, I was shocked because I had never been on a plane. I never had the chance to go to another place. When I got on the plane I didn't know where the bathroom was. I didn't know how to say hello in English because I never went to school. I was just looking around at the white people on the plane. I was scared and thinking maybe they were trying to kidnap us. I was more excited than nervous. I was just with my family trying to be calm and humble. I was trying to remember who I was so I didn't forget my culture.

First we settled in Atlanta, Georgia, for three months. My sister was there already; she came six months before us. She and her friend Mary Helen O'Connor came to the airport and took us to our new home. Mary was helping us adjust to the country. She was fifty years old and a college professor. She had two kids. She took us to many places to visit and helped us with shopping. She taught my oldest brother how to drive. She was the nicest person I have ever met. Mary Helen became my best friend after a while.

I started school, and they put me in seventh grade. I didn't know anything, but I made some friends—Nepali and Latina friends. They were also new, so we were just practicing English together and being friends. Nobody was white, and no one was trying to correct our grammar or anything. We could be just friends.

In Atlanta my dad said, "We're not gonna stay here because we don't know the language and we have no idea what to expect." He had some friends in Minnesota who spoke the language. My dad's friends said, "It's better to be in Minnesota because they have a better education, and we're here to help you guys until you can adjust to the country." There weren't many Somalian people in Atlanta who could help us with the things we needed, and that's why we left after a while. So we came to Minnesota. It was just perfect.

I live in Saint Paul, MN, and I go to LEAP High School. I'm a senior now, and I'm graduating in five months. I want to go to a four-year college and major in nursing or social work. I'm still debating between the two. I want to graduate from college. When I go back to my country, I wanna help people and create jobs. I like to read and write a lot. I have a lot of books about myself. I can just talk about myself all day.

When I was sixteen, my parents kicked me out because they found out that I was gay. After I moved out, I lived in a shelter for several months. I felt lonely and isolated because I have never experienced life alone. I wanted to go back home, so I wrote a letter to my dad. I just wanted to write a letter to let him know how much he meant to me. Over the years, I have been really mean and stubborn. I have always thought he didn't care. However, I know that everyone makes mistakes. With age, I learned that my family is so important. I realized what a helpful family I had. My dad asked me to come back. My family said they missed me, and they promised to never kick me out again. When I came back, everything was okay, and my mom wasn't mad anymore. I think maybe we took some time away and that helped a little. Everything was fine with my family. I spent a lot of time talking about my life with my teachers and my mentors and also with my parents, and that made it easier for me to recover from my stress and depression.

VIDEO LINKS

greencardvoices.org/speakers/nima-ahmed

Acajutla,
El Salvador

Isaac Flores

From: Acajutla, El Salvador
Current City: St. Paul, MN

> "I REMEMBER TRYING AMERICAN FOOD. IT WAS BETTER THAN THE FOOD IN EL SALVADOR. I LIKE THE BUFFETS. WE STILL EAT FOOD FROM EL SALVADOR EVERY DAY AT MY HOUSE. I DON'T LIKE HOW MY FAMILY MAKES IT BECAUSE THERE AREN'T ENOUGH SPICES ON IT."

I am Isaac Flores. I am from Acajutla, El Salvador. I lived my life in El Salvador with my brothers and sisters for eighteen years. There are seven people in my family: my mom, my dad, my two brothers, my two sisters and me. We grew up together. My dad came to America when he was twelve years old. He became a citizen too, and he lived here. Then he moved to El Salvador, but I don't know when. He always told us these stories about him when he was in the US. My dad always told me that someday I might go to America.

A normal day in El Salvador was boring. There was not too much to do. It was too dangerous. My dad didn't like it when we went outside and into the streets because it was too dangerous. But we would always go. We went to the beach to swim and play in the sand. Sometimes my mom would send me to the market to buy food. The market was big and crowded. Acajutla is a big city. It took thirty minutes on my bike to get to the market. Now, in the United States, we shop at Aldi or Walmart. I used to go to a cyber café. You would pay money for Internet or to play video games. I would play video games with my brother at the café. He was better at them. El Salvador has an Independence Day like America. It is on September fifteenth. We set off fireworks and wear the colors of our flag.

I went to a school in El Salvador from first to the ninth grade. It was just across the street from my house. I didn't like the school very much. It was too boring for me. School in El Salvador tries to be like American school, but it doesn't feel like American school. There was one building from first to ninth grade, and then it stops. There is a high school after ninth grade. I did not go to high school in El Salvador because my dad didn't want me to. I played soccer there. It was the only sport I played. I learned how to play the guitar, too. I liked playing classic rock, like Guns N' Roses. I still play soccer and guitar in America.

I remember when we left El Salvador. The economy there was bad. My grandfather, my mother, my little brother, and my little sister took us to the airport. It was my first time in an airplane. Only my sister and I went on the plane. I was eighteen and she was twenty. When the airplane stayed in the air it felt okay. It felt bad when the airplane was descending. It happened twice because we took two airplanes: one plane from El Salvador to Dallas and one from Dallas to Saint Paul. My dad told my grandma to take us to him because only my sister and I had papers to come. I remember that my dad got a little bit angry because we had to leave the house. He was sad and angry at the same time. My dad thought that we were going to be alone without family in Minnesota, but when we arrived my two cousins and my grandma waited for us. It was night when we got to the house. My other family welcomed us. I had seen my cousins before in El Salvador when they were four years old, but I never saw them growing up. Just my grandma. I did not know my aunt and my other aunt and my other cousins.

The first day we were in the United States, I remember that my sister and I felt sad. It felt kind of off balance. In the next few days my family took us to the stores to see and buy things. One time we went to the Mall of America. It was a big mall. My first Minnesota winter wasn't too bad. The first time I saw snow it was actually ice. It was ice on a car window. I like late winter and early spring most in Minnesota. I like that it is not too cold and you get to see the flowers.

I remember trying American food. It was better than the food in El Salvador. I like the buffets. We still eat food from El Salvador every day at my house. I don't like how my family makes it because there aren't enough spices on it. They say it is unhealthy because of the salt. On special days or birthdays we will eat carne asada. It is one of my favorites.

My aunt and my cousin heard about LEAP and took me there. A teacher at LEAP took me to see the school. They put me in a good level because I knew a little bit of English. My dad taught me how to speak a little bit of English. The first day of school felt like it wasn't different from my other school. But now I like this school a little more. I like the art class. We get inspired when we see a view and try to draw. I like to paint landscapes. I like to make things with paper, like paper airplanes. Another subject I like is gym because of the sports we play. I didn't have anything like that in my country. After school I just go home and do homework or play video games. One of my favorite games is Call of Duty. I also like Halo.

In my house now there are five people with me. My uncle and aunt, my two cousins, and me. We live in Saint Paul. My other brothers and sisters are still in El Salvador. My one sister who came to the United States has visited El Salvador since we came here. She is living with her boyfriend now. She is engaged. She still lives in Saint Paul, but far away. I call my mom in El Salvador every day. It is pretty easy to call because Minnesota and El Salvador have the same time. In the summer, El Salvador changes one hour but it's not too tricky to still call.

I am in eleventh grade now. After I graduate from school, I'm going to look for a job. I don't know if I'm going to go to college. But I'm planning to look for a job. Maybe a job with painting houses. I think it would be fun to travel a little. I want to see Las Vegas because it is the city that never sleeps. I want to see that. I will maybe move from the house to live alone or with my girlfriend. I met my girlfriend at LEAP. We have been together for about eleven months. I would like to show her El Salvador and my family. I would also like to visit Mexico with my girlfriend, too. She is from Mexico. I would like to see her family. I would not like to stay in El Salvador. I like living here.

VIDEO LINKS

greencardvoices.org/speakers/isaac-flores

Klopah,
Thailand

Jae Nay Htoo

From: Klopah, Thailand (Karen)
Current City: St. Paul, MN

> "WHEN I WAS IN THE REFUGEE CAMPS, THERE WERE NO SURPRISES IN MY LIFE. IT WAS JUST A SIMPLE LIFE. BUT WHEN I CAME HERE, MANY SURPRISES HAPPENED TO ME, AND THERE WERE MANY CHALLENGES THAT I HAD TO FACE."

I was born in a small village in Thailand, and when I was one year old, my parents moved to a refugee camp called Mae Kaw Kah. I went to kindergarten and finished my first and second grade there. I lived there for like six years, but the flooding destroyed our home and killed many people, so we needed to move to another camp. In 2004, we moved to another camp called Mae La Oon, and I started my teenage life there. I lived with my mom, my grandma, and my brothers. My dad, he didn't stay in the refugee camp; he stayed outside of the refugee camp to find a job and earn money for us. I went to high school there.

My life was so simple and easy. The neighbors that I lived close to were so nice to me, and we would visit each other and have a lot of conversation. It was really fun. I continued my life in Mae La Oon camp year by year until I graduated high school. Sometimes, I felt very low and I was so sick of the same view every day, because I stayed there for a long time. Sometimes I wanted to get out of the camp and discover new things, but I didn't have a chance because I am a refugee and therefore I had a less opportunity to go out of the camp and to do what I want and go where I want to go.

To describe my life in refugee camp, it was going around in a circle, repeating the same thing every day. Even if I stayed in Thailand for ten years or twenty years, I couldn't become a Thai citizen. In order to become Thai citizens, we needed a lot of money, so my family couldn't afford it. However, I feel lucky that I grew up in refugee camp because at least I got to go to school and had teachers to teach me basic English and other subjects. I feel very blessed and grateful for a good life in the refugee camp.

Before my mom applied to the United States, she had to discuss this with my dad because, if we applied, my dad could not follow us because he did not have the UN documents. Because of me, my dad allowed my mom come to the United States only because he wanted me to have a higher education and to discover more about the world.

In 2014, we moved to the United States and I came along with my mom, my grandma, and my brother. We had to take a long bus ride, like eighteen hours, to get to Bangkok. When we got to Bangkok, we slept there one night while waiting to get on our first airplane the next morning to start our long new journey. I remember when I arrived at the Bangkok International Airport, everybody looked at us because they knew we were refugees. Our IOM worker gave us the same jacket, the same shoes, and the same shirt, so we looked a little bit different, and people looked at us. Some people were helpful to us even though we didn't speak their language. They knew that we needed their help, and they came to us to show us the way to the airplane. When people stared at us, I didn't care because I got to see new things and I was very excited to ride the airplane for the first time.

When I first entered the airplane, I was so nervous because I would fly high in the sky, but my excitement was more than my nervousness. I started to feel like my life was already changing in there. The first plane that I took was to fly from Bangkok to Japan, and we changed flights in Tokyo and I took another plane to the Chicago. And there was our last plane, which flew us to Minneapolis.

I have many relatives. They all picked me up from the airport. When I first saw them, I was so excited. I completely forgot about my dad. I forgot about my childhood in Thailand because I was just so excited. I arrived in the nighttime, so I didn't see the outside. For one or two weeks, I could not sleep at night because of the time difference.

After two weeks in Saint Paul, I started my school at LEAP High School. When I first came to school, I saw new people and new culture, and I had to speak English. That was the most difficult obstacle that I had to go through. I started to regret coming to the United States. I started missing my dad, my friends, and Thailand. But I couldn't do anything because I was already here. The only thing that I could do was build more confidence.

I have been here for almost three years. I didn't have any job yet, and I came here because of my education. In my family, I am the youngest. Everybody in my family supported me to have a higher education that none of my family has had before. When I came here, I felt like all people were welcoming me with open arms. I got a free education and I didn't have to walk thirty minutes to go to school. I had a school bus to drive me to school. My daily life has become more colorful and busier than before. When I was in the refugee camps, there were no surprises in my life. It was just a simple life. But when I came here, many surprises happened to me, and there were many challenges that I had to face. I needed to try ten times harder than before to catch up. Two years after we came to the United States, my dad followed us so we could live together again. Two months after my dad arrived in United States, my grandma passed away.

I will graduate this year. I'm the first child in my family who will graduate high school in the US. In the future, after I finish high school, I plan to go to college and become a nurse. I would also like to become a US citizen in the next three years because I want to belong to this country. I plan to become a person who can speak fluent English. In the future I want to help my people who come here and don't speak English very well, and I want to help them to feel more comfortable. I also have another plan. If I have a chance, I want to go back to my country and help my people there. I want to be helpful to other people. Not only my people, but to others too.

VIDEO LINKS

greencardvoices.org/speakers/jae-nay-htoo

Num Hu,
Myanmar

Ah Bay Yan

From: Num Hu, Myanmar (Lisu)
Current City: St. Paul, MN

> "I HAD NEVER IMAGINED THAT I WOULD GO TO THE UNITED STATES. THAT DAY WAS THE BEST DAY OF MY LIFE. WHEN I ARRIVED AT THE AIRPORT, I MET WITH MY RELATIVES, AND I WAS SPEECHLESS."

I was born in a small village called Num Hu. There were about fifty households in the village. I went to school until grade five. I didn't have much privilege in school like I do here. I went to school because my parents forced me to. I walked to school, and I needed to buy school materials on my own, but my parents supported me until grade five. I liked to hang out with my friends and wander in the woods, picking up wild fruit, hunting, and collecting firewood. I used to hunt birds and squirrels, and I brought home those wild animals for food. I didn't really care about school. As I grew up, my life changed. I was not able to go to school and do things that I used to do because I had to help my parents working on farms. My parents grew crops like corn, pumpkins, and many other vegetables. We sold the crops at the market to make some money.

Shooting constantly went on near my village. We often saw the soldiers passing by my village. Sometimes the soldiers just walked into the house and grabbed everything that was useful for them. They took rice, dry meat, and tools like knives. They even threatened villagers. There were some boys taken by soldiers to help them carry things or join in the battles. Since kids disappeared, my parents thought that our life was not safe back in my village, not even in my country, so we decided to move to another country where we could find better lives.

In 2012, when I was fourteen, my family moved to Malaysia. I worked in Malaysia, and we lived there for two years. We went there because we thought we could have better lives. But things didn't turn out like we thought. My mom got caught on the way. Me, my sister, brother, and my dad escaped. We risked our lives to get into Malaysia. Finally, we got into Malaysia. We lived in the capital city of Malaysia, Kuala Lumpur. Yet it was still not safe because we didn't have identification cards or proof that we were legal residents to show to the police, and police were everywhere in the city. We could get caught anytime.

There was an organization that gave aid to the new immigrants. We told them everything that happened to my mom. They gave us cards called the KRC card. It was a member card. This card gave us great relief. If I got caught, I could show the card to the police so they knew that I was a member of the KRC and I would not end up in jail. However, I still needed to pay the police. At first I went to school for a few weeks. The school taught immigrants how to speak English and how to deal with new people. It didn't have many students, and the teaching took place in church. I really liked to go to church. It was a Christian church, and they had a lot of fun activities there.

I started working at a small restaurant. After working there for seven days, I decided to quit because this work was really hard for me. I quit the job without getting paid. The owner would not pay me unless I worked for a month. A few days later, I found a new job. This job was easier and paid well. I liked to work there. I worked in a bakery for six months. Then I needed to find another job because they only needed me for six months in the bakery. I started a new job at a restaurant as a server. I needed to live by myself because my workplace was in the city, two hours away from where my family lived. I started a life by myself. I didn't know what my future held. I woke up early, went to work, came back, and went to bed. This was my daily routine. Things were repeating every day. There was no escape. No supper with family like other kids had. I felt like my mom was a thousand miles away from me. I heard nothing from my mom. All I needed to do was work and support my sister and brother. My dad worked as well, but he had a lot of scars from being caught in a fire, so he worked in a factory. After a year, my mom was released from the prison camp because of the UNHCR's help.

A few months later, we had some interviews at the UNHCR office. The interviews went on for a couple months. Finally, we received our departure date from the UNHCR office. I had never imagined that I would go to the United States. That day was the best day of my life. When I arrived at the airport, I met with my relatives, and I was speechless. We drove to my uncle's apartment, and I was so excited to see the city lights and the view. I couldn't wait to see my other relatives and the place that I was going to live.

At first, we lived in my uncle's place because we couldn't find any available apartments. It was really amazing to see my family and relatives in this new land. I never imagined that this would happen. I got nervous when I first met new people. I was afraid to make eye contact, and I felt embarrassed most of the time when I tried to talk to people. They didn't understand what I said, and they kept asking, "What did you say?" It was really hard for me to understand native speaking. I had to think for a couple minutes about what they said. I got really nervous when I talked to teachers in my school, but slowly it got better because whenever I talked to the teachers, they understood my situation and they tried to make the conversation easier. I know I have a lot of privilege here, and can see my future will be great in this land.

Currently, I'm a student at LEAP High School and I'm going to graduate this year, so I feel happy. Math, physical science, music, and art are my favorite classes. But I like music class the most. I'm taking guitar class as a TA (Teaching Assistant). I help the other students if there is something they don't understand in class. Mostly I play on my own and try to learn something new. I'm working part-time at a restaurant as a server. So I work on Friday and Saturday and sometimes in the evening on weekdays. I go to church every Sunday. We pray, we sing songs, and we listen to the sermons.

I want to move around and see things, explore things, and travel to other states, but I want to stay in Saint Paul because my relatives are all here and it seems like everything's perfect here. I have a plan to go to college after I finish high school. Going to college is a great challenge for me because no one in my family has gone to college. I am the first person who will go to college in my family. Most of my relatives encourage me to take computer science when I go to college because it is a great career, but I'm not sure what I should major in. I went to Saint Paul College once, and it really fascinates me.

VIDEO LINKS

greencardvoices.org/speakers/ah-bay-yan

Tegucigalpa,
Honduras

Tatiana Anariba Osorio

From: Tegucigalpa, Honduras
Current City: St. Paul, MN

"THE FIRST MONTH WITHOUT MY PARENTS WAS A DIFFICULT TIME FOR ME AND MY BROTHERS. NOT SEEING THEM EVERY DAY WAS HARD, ESPECIALLY BECAUSE WE ARE A UNITED FAMILY."

I grew up in Tegucigalpa, the capital of Honduras. I grew up with my whole family: my parents, my brothers, and my sister. I was so lucky because I had everything near my house, like for example, the airport, the malls, and grocer. I was so lucky. My middle school, too, was very close to my house. Things weren't perfect, but they were good.

My grandparents lived close to my house, too, from both sides: my mom's side and my dad's side. I saw them every day. I spent a lot of time talking with them, and it was really fun. I had my aunt, too, really close to my house. I have a big family.

Most of the time, I was in my house helping my mom because she had her own business. I helped clean her hair salon and that kind of stuff. She taught me how to do hair, nails, and makeup.

My dad had his own business, too. It was really nice, but I didn't see him very much because my dad traveled a lot, so I spent most of the time with my mom.

The first person in my family who moved to the United States was my older sister. She moved to the US because she wanted to study and have a better future. My country is a beautiful country, but it's not a safe place to live because the crime is very high. I was afraid to go to school every day. So, every morning my mom would take me to school and then after school my mom would wait for me.

The gangsters started to come to my neighborhood, so it was dangerous to go outside and play with my friends. Five years ago, I lost one of my uncles. The gangsters murdered two members of my family. My parents were really sad about the situation. They were worried about us, so that's why they decided to move to the United States. My sister was really happy about my parents' decision to come to the US.

My parents started to sell everything in our home. My mom went to the United States first, and my father stayed with us. A few months later, my father went to the US. Then, my brothers and I moved to our grandparents' house in Tegucigalpa because we had to be with a guardian. We didn't know how many years we would have to wait for residency papers. I was really sad because I didn't see my parents for more than a year. The first month without my parents was a difficult time for me and my brothers. Not seeing them every day was hard, especially because we are a united family. We had never been separated for that length of time, and to not have my parents by my side made me feel unprotected and unsafe.

I remember when my parents called me and said they had everything ready for me and my little brother. I was a little bit excited and nervous. It was a really good time that day. I remember that my aunts saying, "You have to get ready." I said I had to go and say goodbye to my friends, but my aunts said, "No, you have to pack everything and that's it." I was really sad because I didn't say goodbye to my friends, only to my family. I was crying at the time because I couldn't see my friends for one last time.

When I was in the airport with my family in Honduras, I was crying all the time because I knew I was leaving my family and my friends. I was going to miss the country where I grew up. I was a little bit happy because I would see my parents. When I was in the airplane, my little brother and I flew with a chaperone because we were too young to fly alone. I asked my brother if he was excited to see my parents again and he said, "Yes!"

First I went to Miami and then to Minneapolis. I remember, when I got to Minneapolis, it was 11:00 pm. The first thing that I saw was my parents, my sister, and my nephew. I felt so emotional, and the first thing I did was hug my parents! I was really happy. My mom said we were going to live in St. Paul, and the airport is in Minneapolis, so it is a little far from where we were going to live. So, I said, "Oh, it's okay." My sister drove to our apartment.

At that time it was a little bit hot because it was the summer and I said, "Wow, the weather is really nice," but my mom said, "Wait till the winter. It's really cold here."

When I came to the US, my mom said, "You have to finish your high school. You don't have to worry about working because we want to provide everything for you and your brother. You have to finish high school, study a lot, and that's it." So, I did. Two days later, I started going to high school and saw new people and heard new languages.

My sister found a school for me and my brother. It was LEAP High School. At the time, I didn't know too much English. At LEAP High School, there were a lot of people from different countries. It was perfect to me because I saw many, many students from other countries. I felt very good because I knew they didn't speak very good English, like me.

In the United States, there is only my little brother, my sister, me, my mom, and my dad. In my country is my older brother. I'm not happy because I want my older brother to come to the US and stay with us and live with us.

I have a part-time job on weekends. Most of the time I'm in school. I'm taking nursing assistant classes right now, so I'm really excited about that. I want to finish high school and I want to go to college. Before I go to college, I want to improve my English and my writing. I want to study to become a dentist. That's one of my goals. I also want to own a hair salon with my family.

VIDEO LINKS

greencardvoices.org/speakers/tatiana-anariba-osorio

Tak,
Thailand

Sha Lay Paw

From: Tak, Thailand (Karen)
Current City: St. Paul, MN

"WE HAD TO TAKE AN AIRPLANE CLASS TO LEARN WHAT TO DO ON AN AIRPLANE. LIKE HOW TO BUCKLE THE SEATBELT. I DIDN'T WANT TO GO ON AN AIRPLANE."

My mom lived in Myanmar. She had to work so hard just to eat, so she decided to go to the Umpiem Mai refugee camp in Thailand.

It was a difficult trip. She had three kids with her, and she was pregnant; I was in her stomach. I was born on the border of Myanmar and Thailand. My dad disappeared when they were going to the refugee camp. We never saw him again.

It was difficult for my mother because she was the only person my siblings and I had. It was difficult for her to work, so she sent my sister to a boarding school. She was ten. It was free for her to go. My mom sent my brothers to a school that was far from us. My mom had to leave me and my sisters behind so she could work outside of the camp. We lived with our aunt. I was five years old. I went to school, but I did not like it. I didn't have any money to buy lunch, and since my aunt wasn't my mother, it was difficult for me to ask for money.

After a year, my mom came back to the refugee camp. The day she came back, my stepdad said, "Guess who is in the house laying in the bed?" I was scared, but I pulled back the covers and it was my mom! I was so happy. She brought back peanuts that she boiled and put salt on. They were really good. When my mom came back, she worked on a farm in the camp every day. I wanted to help her, but she wanted me to focus on my education. She didn't want me to work on a farm like her. She risked her life to get me a good education because she wanted me to have a better life and be successful.

When my sister was sixteen, she came back from school. She said she heard people were going to the United States. She told my mom she wanted to go there for a better education, a better life. At first my mom didn't want to go to the United States because she didn't understand the language. My sister

49

said that she knew English and Thai and she would help my mom.

I had no idea what they were saying. I had never heard of the United States. I was young then and just wanted to play in the forest with my brother. My mother didn't want us to play there, but we would sneak out to see the waterfalls, eat fruits from the high trees, and play.

At first we had to go to get our UN picture, and then we had an interview. And then we went to another place to get a shot and to get ready to go to the United States. We stayed there a month. We had to take an airplane class to learn what to do on an airplane, like how to buckle the seatbelt. I didn't want to go on an airplane. I was even scared to ride in a car because I was afraid I would fly out. I wasn't sure what it would feel like on the airplane. When I was on the airplane, the food tasted so nasty because that's not what I usually ate.

We went to Utah and lived there a month. One of my sister's teachers from the boarding school was in Michigan, so we moved there. My mom and dad always argued, and the social worker said that it would be dangerous for us children to live with our parents so they separated us from our mom and dad. My sister and I lived with an American couple, and my two brothers went to another family. I hated it so much. The first night I cried, and cried, and cried. After six or seven months they wanted to adopt us. My mom decided she didn't want us to be adopted. She asked a priest to help us. He was from Connecticut, so we moved there.

We lived in Connecticut for three years. My mom and stepdad separated, and she didn't want to live there anymore. My youth leader, who was pastor, was from Minnesota. He said there is a Karen community, and he told my mom there would be better care and if she moved there, he would take responsibility for her.

We moved to Minnesota in 2013. I started to learn English in Michigan. I was so scared and confused, but on my first day of school they treated me nice. My friend—she was adopted by an American—knew Karen and English, so I used her as an interpreter. In Connecticut, I went to a middle school. The immigrant students were discriminated against; students bullied us because we didn't know English. Now I am at LEAP High School. When I came to LEAP High School, I felt like I belonged here. LEAP is a diverse place, but everyone is treated equally. I like the teachers very much. They are supportive and know how you are feeling.

Before I went to LEAP High School, I didn't know what I was going to do in the future. I didn't have any hope. But at LEAP High School I've learned better English, and I see my future. I don't really know exactly what I want to be, but I know I want to continue my education.

Someday I want to have a beautiful family, and I want to travel. I think I will travel back to where my mom grew up. I want to go back and see what everything looks like.

VIDEO LINKS

greencardvoices.org/speakers/sha-lay-paw

Ginchi,
Ethiopia

Yomiyu Gafesu

From: Ginchi, Ethiopia (Oromo)
Current City: St. Paul, MN

"I WANNA WORK IN A HEALTH AREA, ESPECIALLY WITH THE CHILDREN—NOT ONLY IN ETHIOPIA BUT IN DIFFERENT PLACES AS MUCH AS I CAN."

I grew up in a town called Ginchi, in the Oromia region. It is close to our capital city, Addis Ababa, and it is a small town. I lived there for about eighteen years with my parents and my siblings. The town is very small, so I know many of the people in there. We were all very close. I went to school there until grade ten, and I had a lot of friends. We went to school together since we were children because we only had one school, and I really had a good time there. My family was really supportive even though life wasn't perfect. My parents took care of me and all of my brothers and sisters, and they gave us what every child needs. It was good. Other than going to school, I played with my friends. We went to church. There, most of them are Orthodox Christian, and we practiced in a church. Also, I helped my mom at home, doing things like cooking, cleaning, and helping my brother with studying.

I'm not the one who decided to come here. My dad came before us in 2011 because of my uncle. Then he stayed here. I thought he would come back, but he told us that he decided to stay here and bring his family here. Then he started the process. I just remember back after a year or something like that he informed us that we were ready to come here. At that time, I was really excited because I knew a little about this country. I was sure that my dreams could come true. And I felt like, "Yes, I can be the kind of person I want to be," because in Ethiopia even if you have a degree or education, it is really hard to find the job you want.

The political situation is not very good back there. My family wasn't accepted or liked because they didn't like the government, and the government didn't give us the rights every human should have, such as the right to speak and to do what we want to do. Many people have been killed and thrown in prison because they opposed the administration. My parents always wanted us to have a better, brighter future. That's why my dad decided to bring us here. So I was happy when he informed us, but it was not for all of us. Five of my siblings are still in Ethiopia.

After our process started, I thought it would be finished very soon, but it took a while. We were kind of stressed because, as I said, my town is very small and everyone knew we were going to come to the US. So when it took a while and there were a lot of challenges, everybody asked, "Why? Why? What happened to your process? Why is your father not coming back?" It was really stressful and everyone asked questions, and it affected us. Our school, too, knew that I was going to come here. I started to get very low grades, and I didn't like school as much as I did in elementary school. A lot of things pushed me down and that was a very bad time. The embassy called us, and they said we were permissioned, and then I was really excited. They gave us our visa. Then, after a month, we packed everything, and we came. It wasn't very happy for me because I had to leave a lot of things there, like my siblings, my nieces and nephews, my grandparents, and our village.

I traveled with my mom and four siblings. When we traveled to the United States, our uncle was with us. He came to Ethiopia for vacation. He lives here. He was with us, so we weren't very confused at the airport. He was the one who opened this big opportunity for us and, using this opportunity, I want to thank him. It was a little bit scary on the plane because it was my first time, but it wasn't as I expected. It was good. We traveled with our uncle, and he helped us with what we had to do at the airport.

First, we landed in Washington, and our second plane landed in Minneapolis. I thought there would be a few people, like my dad and some of my relatives, but when I landed here, there were a lot of people. There were white people that my dad knew. I was really panicked at that time. I was really happy when I saw my dad after five years. I was surprised by a lot of things. Before we came, my dad told us what it was going to be like. He said, "It might not be how you expect it." It is not how I expected. You know when people say "the United States," my mind thinks something like, Oh, heaven! But there are a lot of obstacles here also. He told us about the weather. When I came here it wasn't very cold, but for me it was cold, but after a month or something like that, the winter started. The winter was really hard.

The second challenging thing was language. I understand a little bit, but it was hard for me to speak up. I was on a train and someone asked me something, I don't remember what it was, and I was trying to respond to them, but my English wasn't perfect and the people who sat behind me kind of laughed at me. I went home and cried, and I said, "How can I go to school, and how can I face this country?" but I went to a good school. I am going to a good school, so it's not that hard now. It's getting better for me.

I've been here for one year and four months. Now I go to LEAP High School. I was very scared because this was my first time dealing with different people, but it wasn't that hard because our school is very diverse. They put me in little upper level, and I was kind of scared. English challenged me, but after a few months, I'm getting better and better. Now I don't have any extra things to do. Like, I don't have any job. I mostly stay at home. On the weekend I go to church. I help my family at home. They work now. I help them by cooking and cleaning stuff. I participate in different leadership programs. Last year I was in leadership called GGAL. This year I'm in a leadership program called Youth Leadership Initiative. Right now, something I wanna do is focus on my school and get good grades. That's what I want.

I love science. I wanna become a pediatrician. I love children, so I wanna work with them. In our country, the health care is not good. We don't have enough nutrition. Every child needs good food and a good education. After I finish high school, I wanna go to college. Then after a year of experience, I wanna go back home if the government becomes good or changes. I wanna work in a health area, especially with the children—not only in Ethiopia but in different places as much as I can.

VIDEO LINKS

greencardvoices.org/speakers/yomiyu-gafesu

GET LUCKY

TEAM 7K ORTHO

SENTED BY

Kieran's
Irish
Pub

Yangon,
Myanmar

Christ Taw

From: Yangon, Myanmar (Karen)
Current City: St. Paul, MN

"SOMETIMES I WOULD SNEAK OUT OF THE CAMP WITH MY FRIENDS AND GO OUT TO THE FOREST TO FIND SOME FOOD. SOMETIMES WE WOULD FIND VEGETABLES AND SOMETIMES WE WOULD HUNT ANIMALS."

I was born in Burma. When I was one month old, my parents moved to Thailand. I stayed in Thailand for thirteen years. I went to school there from kindergarten to fourth grade. Then I came to the US when I was thirteen.

I was in a camp in Thailand. My family was all together in the camp. We are all still together today. There are five people in my family: my mom, my dad, my brother, my sister, and me. I had a lot of friends in the camp. We would go to school together, go to the river and swim, and play together. Some of them came to the US too. In the camp you could leave, but you always needed permission. You would ask the government to go into the city and they would say yes or no. You could leave to work or go to school. I had to walk to school.

School started at 8:30 a.m. We would go home for lunch and then go back to school until two. Sometimes I would stay after school and watch people play soccer. It was a pretty big school. There were maybe three thousand people there. It was first through tenth grade. I liked going to school. I did not like the teachers so much. They would use a stick if you didn't do your homework and they would hit you. Sometimes you would have to run around the school. I used to do that a lot. We had to pay money for school. Fourth grade cost me two hundred baht for one year. I stopped going to school after fourth grade because it was too expensive. It was hard to find money. There weren't many jobs and if you had a job you had to walk two days to get to work. My mom and dad would make only thirty to fifty baht a day.

There were other places in the camp to go to. There were many churches there. There also were missionaries. A lot of churches and missionaries in the camp. Each section would have different churches. I went to the churches a lot. There was also a library and a hospital there. I would go to the library a lot and read stories a lot. I like reading funny stories and books about history. I read a lot about other countries' histories.

Life was kind of hard in the camp. There was not a lot of food. Sometimes I would sneak out of the camp with my friends and go out to the forest to find some food. Sometimes we would find vegetables and sometimes we would hunt animals. We would see many animals like birds, deer, and squirrels. If you stayed in the forest, it was crazy. It was dangerous. I saw a lot of snakes in the forest, like cobras. I also saw a water snake. The snakes could kill you. If they bit you, you were gonna die. When I saw the snakes, I would run away.

My parents decided to come to the US. They wanted to come here to have a better life and they wanted me to have a better life and a better future. People from the UN came to the camp and told us we could apply to come to the US. They helped us figure out how to apply to come. All of my family went to an interview. After the interview, we stayed in the camp for three months. There was body check to make sure we were healthy.

We all left together. First, we had to take a car to Thailand. We stayed for one week, and then we took another bus to Bangkok. We stayed one night in a hotel then went to the airport. We took airplanes from Thailand to Japan and Japan to New York. We stayed one night in New York and then took an airplane from New York to Minnesota. When we arrived in Saint Paul, my caseworker and my father's friends were waiting at the airport. The caseworker took me to the apartment of my father's friend, and we stayed there for one week. My father's friends came to help us a little bit when we first came to America and when we moved to our apartment. The caseworker gave my family a bag and some other stuff. He gave my parents some food and some money. After one week in the apartment, the caseworker got us a new apartment. We stayed in that apartment for seven months. After that, we left because there was another apartment that was with my other family. There aren't a lot of my people in the new apartment.

The first days in Minnesota were strange. Everything was new. This place was different from my home country. I had not seen a refrigerator before. There were a lot of cars. People had a lot of different cars. There were a lot of tall buildings and traffic. The first time I saw snow was in Minnesota. I like the snow, but I do not like the cold. I like summer more.

I did not know English before coming to America. I spoke a little Burmese and knew Karen, and then I learned English in the US. When I first saw Karen people here, I felt happy. Some of my neighbors are from the same camp. We all came to Minnesota at different times when our interviews passed. Two family members are in Minnesota. They live close to us. My uncles and cousins are still there in the same camp we were. They still get to talk to us on the phone. I would like to go back to visit Thailand and see them.

I am a senior in high school. I have been in school here for five years. My favorite subject is writing. I like to write journals. I play all different sports. I like soccer the most. On the weekend, I go to the movie theater. Sometimes I just stay home and watch movies and eat. We watch American movies and Chinese Kung fu movies. Also, when I am not at school, I like fishing. I catch catfish and sunfish. I mostly fish in a lake or in the Minnesota River. When we go fishing we use worms to catch fish. Sometimes we use bread. The biggest fish I caught was a catfish a few years ago. After I catch the fish, I just bring it home and my family cooks it. In the summer, I go fishing and have barbeques in the park with my friends. We hang out and do many different things and go many different places.

In the future, I will stay in Saint Paul. After I finish high school I think I'm going to go to college. Then I want to be a mechanic. I want to be a mechanic because I want to have my own business where I can help the people in my neighborhood. I want to have a place where my people have someone to talk to for help with their cars.

VIDEO LINKS

greencardvoices.org/speakers/christ-taw

Tak,
Thailand

Say Hay Taw

From: Tak, Thailand (Karen)
Current City: Austin, MN

"I FELT EXCITED AND SAD AT THE SAME TIME. THE FIRST TIME I FELT IT WOULD BE REALLY HARD LIVING IN THE US. BUT THE MORE I LIVE HERE. IT BECOMES EASIER. "

My name is Say Hay Taw. I am sixteen years old. I am Karen and from Thailand. My parents are from Myanmar.

I was born in Thailand, and I grew up there. I don't have a lot of friends left there. It's kind of a scary place because sometimes a lot of Thai people came in and asked for our food, so we had to give them our food. If we didn't give them food, they punished us.

I was born in a Thai refugee camp. It's called Mae Ra Moe, and there are a lot of Karen people that lived far away from each other. The camp is not too big.

I went to No. 3 High School, and I studied there to fourth grade but I failed. I had to study fourth grade two times, but I still failed it the second time, too.

When I woke up Monday mornings, I went to school and came back and helped my mom feed a pig or chicken. In my camp, we didn't have a school bus, so I always walked to and back from school. Saturdays, we went off from the camp looking for food. We went far away, like two hours, looking for bamboo shoots and banana flowers and other food.

Sometimes, I went out with my friends. Sometimes, we went swimming in the big river. My parents didn't want me to swim in the big river, but I didn't listen to them. If they knew that I went to swim in the river, they would hit my butt with bamboo sticks. I always had to go sneak out so I could go swim.

The day I found out I was coming to the US, I didn't tell any teachers in my school. I didn't let them know. For one week, I didn't go to school, and then they knew it. I didn't want them to feel bad. The teachers were nice. Almost all of my friends already left to other countries. The day I found out I was coming to the United States, I only had two friends left, but I had to leave them. I felt very sorry for them.

We started going to Bangkok by car. Then we got off there and got on a big bus, and then they dropped us off at Bangkok. We got off there. They gave us food, and we slept there overnight. Early in the morning, they took us to an airplane. We flew all the way to Japan. Then, we switched to another airplane. We flew all the way to Chicago. We switched to another plane and flew to the Saint Paul airport.

When we arrived in Minnesota, there were some relatives waiting for me and my family in the airport. I felt excited and sad at the same time. The first time I felt it would be really hard living in the US, but the more I live here, it becomes easier.

The first time I saw snow I loved it. Every day I went outside with my sister and played with snow. When I go to the store, I just look for food I like. I don't buy food I don't like. I only buy Asian food.

The first time I saw flowers and trees blooming, I thought I lived in another country, but it is still the United States. I just went outside with my sisters, and we took a lot of pictures. I love blooming flowers and blooming trees.

I came to the US when I was twelve years old. I didn't know how to speak English. I went to Four Seasons A+ Elementary. I was the only Karen girl in my classes. The first day I went to school, I felt sad and lonely because I had no friends. The second day of school I felt more confident. I tried to talk to other people. I still felt sad, but I controlled my tears. The third day of school, I felt like I just wanted to cry. I couldn't control my tears so I cried in front of the classmates.

I graduated from sixth grade. I moved to a different school called Linwood Monroe Arts Plus. After I graduated from eighth grade, I moved to LEAP High School.

I have lived in St. Paul for four years. I just moved down to Austin one month ago. I didn't want to move but I had to. I moved to Austin because my parents bought a house and I have to live with them because I am not eighteen yet.

High school in Austin is different than in St. Paul. There are more people in Austin High School but not a lot of Karen people. A few but not a lot. Austin High School is three times bigger than LEAP High School.

At LEAP High School, I didn't see a lot of white people. Most of the teachers were white, but not the students. Mostly the students are color people or Asian. But they were nice. Same as the Austin students, too.

In LEAP High School, they didn't have sports or other programs; they only have after-school programs. I stayed after school two days a week to learn more English. The teacher helps us with our homework.

Two of my sisters are still living in St. Paul. The others are living with my family. It is hard to see each other. Sometimes she goes there and visits us on the weekend.

VIDEO LINKS

greencardvoices.org/speakers/say-hay-taw

El Aguacatal,
El Salvador

Cristina Vasquez

From: El Aguacatal, El Salvador
Current City: St. Paul, MN

"I USED TO WORK WITH MY UNCLES ON A FARM, GROWING TOMATOES, GREEN BEANS, AND THINGS LIKE THAT... IT WAS HARD, BUT I REALIZED I HAD TO WORK TO HELP MY MOM AND TO BE INDEPENDENT."

I was born in El Salvador, in a small town called El Aguacatal. It is small. It has around maybe one hundred people. We are all almost family. My mom left me when I was one year old because she had to work to give me a better life. Then when I was five, my mom had my brother and she went to live with his father. But when my brother was ten months old, his father died. He was sick. Then, she had to bring my brother to my grandparents' home. She stayed a couple days and then left to go to work. She gave a notice that she was leaving to come to the US. Later when I was ten, she moved to the United States. She didn't have enough money for us to come with.

I grew up with my grandparents, uncles, and aunts. I used to work with my uncles on a farm, growing tomatoes, green beans, and things like that. The farm was forty minutes from my home. I would take a car with my uncles to go to the farm. Sometimes I would not go to work with them, but I would bring lunches. My grandma would make the food and then I would bring it. My grandfather also had a farm at our house. He grew granadillas. I would help him cut the fruit on the tree. We would put the fruit in crates and bring it to the market. It was hard, but I realized I had to work to help my mom and to be independent. It was kind of hard for me because I was little. My uncles paid me when I worked with them. I was excited, because then I had my own money. I could buy things.

Then, I went to school. I had to walk a lot to get there. It was big. The school would move because they needed kids to be there. There were kids at the school, but then they moved, so the school closed in my town. Later a new school was built in my town. It wasn't a real school. It was just like a room like at LEAP. I did not hang out with a lot of people my age because I was with my grandparents all the time. There was a path to school where we had to walk through a creek. When we came back, we would have to get clean in a *poza de agua* because we were sweaty and dirty from the creek.

When my mom arrived here, we used to communicate by calling. She called me and I called her almost every day because she missed me and my brother and we missed her. Later we decided for me to come, and I was excited because I never lived with her and I thought this would be a great opportunity for me to be with her. She was already here with my sister—she was two years old—and I said, "Oh my gosh!" I would be with my little sister. I came to America when I was sixteen years old.

I was so excited, but when I came here it was difficult for me. It was kind of cold and I thought Oh my God, here it is too cold. But when the snow came I was excited. I'd never seen snow before. It was fun, but at the same time, it was cold. My life became more difficult because I came in October and the weather got colder.

When I was first in America, my mom, my uncles, and I all lived together. A year and a half later, my mom moved to another house, so I had to live with my uncles. I still live with my uncles. I had to pay for everything by myself. At the beginning, it was hard for me. But then it became easier because now I'm independent for everything. It is very important for me to realize how hard life is.

I think I'd been in America for two weeks when my dad came to my house. I was so excited to see him because he left to America when my mom was pregnant. He would sometimes call and send pictures when I was in El Salvador, but a picture is never the same as the real person.

The language and the food were so hard for me, especially the language. We still make meals from El Salvador every day, but it tastes very different. My mom doesn't speak much English, but she told me to go to school to learn the language. Then my life would become easier. "That way, you can have a better job than the one I had," and things like that.

At beginning of the school year it was hard for me because there were many Latin people in my school, but in my classes, there were no people who speak Spanish. It was hard at the beginning, but at the same time it helped me a lot to learn the language a little bit faster. Then my English, my speaking, and my writing grew more because I did my best and my teachers helped me a lot to improve my English. When I'd been in school for two weeks, a girl from Ecuador arrived. She didn't speak English as well as me. We started to help each other, and we became best friends. So in a way our life became easier. I'm doing my best to learn English more.

When I am done with school at four o'clock I take a bus. Then, I go to my work, and when I get there, I do almost everything. Cashier, cook, clean. I get off between ten and midnight, and sometimes I get tired, but I say I have to work because I want to keep going to school until I graduate and go to college.

On the weekends, usually on Saturdays, I wake up late because I am tired from Friday. Sometimes I have to do laundry, and I go on Saturdays. On Sundays, I usually go to church with my uncles. My grandparents always taught us to go to church when we were little, and we still do. Then when I am done with church I come home or go to the restaurant and have something to eat. Then I later have to go to work.

My life is easier now because I have my own job and my own money. It helped me a lot, and I became independent. My hopes for the future are to graduate from high school, go to college, and have good education. I'm thinking about becoming a nurse or lawyer. I hope I can get the degree from college. I'm wondering if in the future I will go back to El Salvador or visit because I miss my grandparents. It's hard for me because I grew with them. Especially my grandma. I still call them when I can and help them. I want to see them again and to meet with my other family members that were born when I was here. I'm wondering if I can visit them, but my life is still here. I want to be here, because here is more easy than my life there.

VIDEO LINKS

greencardvoices.org/speakers/cristina-vasquez

Phnom Penh,
Cambodia

Huoy Lin Mao

From: Phnom Penh, Cambodia
Current City: St. Paul, MN

"I LIKE TO READ THE NEWS IN THE NEWSPAPER AND ONLINE. I WANT TO KNOW ABOUT WHAT IS HAPPENING ON THE OUTSIDE AND WHAT OTHER PEOPLE ARE DOING."

Almost sixteen years ago, I lived in Cambodia. I went from my country to Cambodia. My mom and my dad have been divorced since I was ten years old. My mom moved here in 2008. I spent time living with my dad. My life's not bad. I like it. My dad teaches children up to grade six. I would go to school with my dad. He brought me and he taught me like any other student. My brother lived with my grandmother.

I had four friends from high school in Cambodia. High school was grade seven to twelve. Some people went to college, and I came here. When I came here, I started at grade nine. We took the motorcycle or a bicycle to school. We didn't have a bus. My favorite subject in my country was reading and history of my country. Here the history is more law and government.

In 2013, my mother and I left to go visit my grandma in Cambodia. The lawyer called to tell her that I could come with her. She could support me to come with her to the United States. My mom married a new husband and came here first. In 2013, when I went back with her, my grandma passed away. I came here with my mom and the new lady and my brother on February 27, 2013. My dad came with me to the airport. We cried a lot. We didn't want to come, but it was a long time never staying with my mom.

I got to visit him last year. I traveled by myself alone to visit him. He was so surprised. When I went, I didn't plan to tell him first. I told nobody, and when I got to his job they said, "He's not here." But I gave a letter to his class, and when he came back, he found the letter I signed. I put my phone number on it for him, and he called me and he said, "Where's your brother?"

And I said, "He's not coming."

He asked me why my brother was not coming. It was because he was still in high school. I didn't want to make him come and lose his high school credit. But dad still misses my brother. We cannot always go together because my mom's scared. She says, "Next time, when he finishes high school."

I went back to my country and surprised everybody in 2015. That was nice. I stayed two months to visit my dad, my grandma, my grandpa. We went to temples for my culture and religion. The month I planned for my birthday, I spent time with my dad.

Everything here is different a lot from my country. I was sixteen. It's been over four years now, so I'm twenty-one. When I first saw the snow, I was so surprised, and I told mom, "This place is very nice." We had a lot of problems speaking and understanding some people. We had never spoken English before. I didn't have friends that spoke Cambodian, so it was hard. But now I can speak English a little bit. Not too much, not well. I got a job, and my manager taught me how to speak better. Now my mom sometimes says I talk too fast.

I work at the airport in the place where they make the food to put on the airplane. My house is near the place where I work. It's just a ten minute drive. It's six days a week, but on Fridays we only work five hours and Sundays we work seven. We cook and clean, and we close the kitchen. It is so busy on Monday or Friday. We work three or four hours and get a fifteen-minute break.

I spend the whole day at work and school. Some days I finish school after seven hours, and I spend five hours at my job. The whole day is busy. I stay after school to take one more class, Geometry II, for graduation.

I like funny books, fiction books, and the magazines about clothes, houses, and makeup. I like to read the news in the newspaper and online. I want to know about what is happening on the outside and what other people are doing. I read in Khmer and in English. I can still read and write in Khmer.

This is the last year of school for me. This year, in the springtime I have a lot of time because of graduation. And after graduation, I will apply and go to college. Before I go to college, I want to spend my time to work full time to make money and to pay for college. Maybe I will find a new job. I want to bring my brother to surprise my dad too.

My mom wants me to go to college and learn to be a nurse. That's the dream for my mom. Because she says she's always sick, and she wants me to be is a nurse so I can check on her. But I just want to make her dreams come true. I wanted to finish college in my country before I came. But I couldn't, so I'll start from here.

VIDEO LINKS

greencardvoices.org/speakers/huoy-lin-mao

Ban Mae Ook Hu,
Thailand

Eh Sa Kaw

From: Ban Mae Ook Hu, Thailand (Karen)
Current City: St. Paul, MN

> "I'D LIKE TO GO BACK TO MY HOME COUNTRY AND SEE MY FAMILY THERE. I PLAN A LOT TO TRAVEL AROUND THE WORLD. I WISH TO TRAVEL AROUND EVERY COUNTRY."

My parents come from Burma. They moved to Thailand because of the civil war just to have freedom. My parents didn't have an opportunity to get any education. I lived in a village called Ban Mae Ook Hu. I had a lot of friends. I went to school starting in the first grade all the way to fourth. School was the same, except you had to buy your own books sometimes. The teacher taught us Thai. My parents don't know how to speak Thai. My dad can speak Burmese, Karen, and Pokaren, which is similar to Karen. My mom just speaks Karen, but she sometimes understands Burmese and Pokaren a little bit. Life there was hard because my parents didn't have jobs. It was hard to find a job. They didn't have money to send me to school. We didn't have any free time at all. We were not Thai citizens, so they asked for ID and money to visit other villages.

In Thailand, I liked to draw. I drew around my village. I drew landscapes, some animals, and a beautiful ocean. Sometimes I liked to go fishing and swimming in the lake and river. You can jump into the river from a bridge.

We moved to the United States because there is more freedom and my parents wanted me to have a good education and make money easily. Wherever my parents go, I go with them. They just told me to pack your bag and I'm like, "Okay." Then we went to Bangkok before we went to the airport. We slept in a hotel in Bangkok and then in the morning we started packing up again then went to the airport and took a plane to Japan and then one to America in the same day. We arrived in New York at night. It was kind of rainy there and cold. I was feeling hungry, tired, and cold. I stayed in New York for one night in a hotel. Then in the morning we took the flight to Indiana.

My first day in the US, I already wanted to go back to Thailand. I thought it was always gonna be cold in this country because it was winter time. When I came to Indiana I just felt lonely. I didn't have any friends. I didn't know where to go. I just lay on the bed thinking about school and family in Thailand. I lived in an apartment near car racing. It was loud, and a lot of people came and watched.

I started school in eighth grade. The first day in school was the worst day. I had no friends. All I saw was a Spanish-speaking student. They thought I also spoke Spanish, so they tried to speak to me. I said, "What? No. What kind of language is that?" When we wanted to go to the store or hospital, we needed a translator or interpreter. There were few Karen people there, and it was hard for my dad. That is why he wanted to move to Minnesota.

We lived in Indiana for nine months, and then we came to Saint Paul. I was fifteen when we came here. I like Minnesota. I met a lot of Karen people. I met my cousin's family, who I never met in Thailand. I have seven siblings—four sisters and three brothers. My second sister lives here. She has three babies, all girls, and my older sister lives in Thailand and has two babies, both boys. The third sister lives in another state—Missouri. Right now I just live with my dad and mom. I like it. There are no kids, so it's quiet. Sometimes there are kids in the apartment, and they annoy me. I will live with my parents until I get married. I am the youngest son, and no one else will take care of them. I'm the only one who will take care of them when they get older. I will invite them to live with me because my sister already moved out.

LEAP was my second school. Humboldt was my first school when I moved here. It was kind of bad. There was too much fighting. I never fight or make trouble in school. I like LEAP. The teachers are all kind and respectful. I like our automotives class and I don't like math. A lot of people are friendly and the classes are helpful, and they help you with college scholarships and applications. I'm taking the SAT and applying for Saint Paul College.

In Minnesota, I like to draw people and animals. I never play sports, but after school I go to gym and come home to my work. When I was little, I followed my father everywhere, even when he went to the temple to worship. Now, my parents invite me, but I don't want to go.

I'm planning to go to college for two years or maybe four years, and I want to study to be an auto mechanic. I want to own a dealership and have my own company. I will complete all that hard work before I get the job. I've been thinking and talking about travel a lot. I'd like to go back to my home country and see my family there. I plan a lot to travel around the world. I wish to travel around every country. First, I want to go to Hawaii. They have beautiful beaches and volcanoes. And second, after Hawaii, I want to go to Thailand and taste all the street food. I will save money first before I travel. I'll come back to Minnesota and work here. That's what I plan in my future.

VIDEO LINKS

greencardvoices.org/speakers/eh-sa-kaw

Mogadishu, Somalia

Aisha Abdullahi

From: Mogadishu, Somalia (Somali)
Current City: St. Paul, MN

> "SAINT PAUL WAS DIFFERENT—THE PEOPLE, THE HOUSES, THE BUILDINGS. I DIDN'T KNOW ANYTHING. I DIDN'T SPEAK ENGLISH."

My name is Aisha Adbullahi, and I was born in Somalia. I grew up with my grandma and my sister. People say I am quiet and shy and unique. I am nineteen; I was sixteen years old when I moved here. I didn't grow up with my mother because she was already in the United States. Or my siblings, because they were already here. My oldest sister—her name is Sacdiyo— is twenty. My youngest brother, Yacqub, is two. My other sisters are Zaynab, Fatima, and Amina. I have four sisters and four brothers, so that is eight.

I went to school back home, but I didn't really care that much because I didn't know that it was important. Sometimes I went to go to school and sometimes I skipped. School was different; teachers wouldn't worry if we skipped. About three hundred people were in the school. We studied math, reading, writing, and science. I was in the ninth grade when I came here. But when I came here, I noticed that school is important and all that. I used to go to the mosque, read my Quran, and learn. My grandparents just encouraged me to do my best at school and study hard. Other times we just stayed home. It was not hard to live there. We lived in a city, I think. I miss living in Somalia. I miss how it looks and my friends and my grandmother. Sometimes it is hot, sometimes it is warm and it rains. I miss that.

When I was little, not real little, my grandma told us to buy ice because she was fasting. My sister and I went to buy the ice, but we just didn't come home for a long time, so my grandma got worried. We just went to a friend's house to watch a movie. We came home at night and the ice was melted. We had lied about where we went, we told her the ice machine wasn't working, but she found out. My grandma was angry at me, and she told us we weren't going to go anywhere for a long time. She just said it to scare us.

One day they told us we were moving to Minneapolis, and then we had to pack. First we went to Kenya— my grandparents had reasons to go there—and then we came straight to the US. My mom came to get us. It had been a long time since I'd seen her. I was little, so I don't remember. I didn't talk to her much. When we came to the airport, we said goodbye to the grandparents. And we just left.

On the airplane, I was scared. When we arrived, my dad and my other siblings came to the airport to take us home, and we just went home and celebrated. We ate food and we talked for quite a while. Saint Paul was different—the people, the houses, the buildings. I didn't know anything. I didn't speak English. I arrived in winter, around December, and it was very cold. I was very happy to see my younger brothers and sisters.

When we first arrived in the US, we stayed home for like month, and then we started going to mosque. The first month we would just go shopping and stay at home. The shops were different and interesting. In Somalia, there are only small ones, and here there are big ones. After one month, we started school, and then everything was different. I went to a mixed school. There were some Somali students, but not a lot. I think I kind of liked the mixed school. It was a charter school. Then I came to LEAP and everything was the same as the mixed school, but the students were different. I like the teachers at LEAP and how they help the students. I miss my friends from Somalia. I don't like the cold; I like snow, but it's too cold.

After school, I just stay at home and hang out with my siblings. Sometimes I help them with their homework, watch TV, and clean. My dad works day and night, and my mom works in the morning. I like the neighbors and how close they are in the building. If we need something, we can just knock on the door. The Mall of America has a movie theater, and I like the movie theater. I like all kinds of movies except horror movies. I like watching movies with someone, not by myself.

This is my last year. I'm graduating. I think I want to go to college and study to be a nurse. I just like to help people and make a difference in the community. I will go to college right away after I graduate. Century has a good nursing program. I want to work with sick and older people. I like babies, but they cry too much and I worry, so I want to work with older people. After I graduate LEAP, I will work part-time in the Air Service. I am working on being a certified nursing assistant now at LEAP. In June, we are going to take a state test, and if I pass maybe I will become a nurse. Sometimes it is easy and sometimes it's hard.

I want to stay in Minnesota and be a nurse here. My family is here, and I can leave with them to travel. My mom's friend usually goes to Dubai to visit. She showed us pictures of it, and it is beautiful. I liked the beautiful buildings and houses. And I want to go back to my country and visit my grandparents and my friends. I talk to them on the phone. I miss them. I hope to travel to India. But I want to stay in Minnesota for now because after many years, all my family is all together and in one house.

VIDEO LINKS

greencardvoices.org/speakers/aisha-abdullahi

Yangon,
Myanmar

Oh Kler

From: Yangon, Myanmar (Karen)
Current City: St. Paul, MN

> "I HAD TO WALK TO SCHOOL BECAUSE WE DIDN'T HAVE SCHOOL BUSES. MOST PEOPLE COULD NOT PAY FOR ELECTRICITY. WHEN I STUDIED FOR A TEST AT NIGHT, I WOULD USE A CANDLE."

My name is Oh Kler. I am Karen, and this is my immigration story. I was born in a village in Burma. At that time there were four people in my family. I am the oldest child. My parents were farmers, and we all lived together. Life in Burma was not easy for a couple of reasons. One big problem was that we had to pay taxes to the Burmese government, and my parents didn't have the money to pay. If you couldn't pay the money, or refused to pay, the government could force you to become a Burmese soldier. Boys usually became soldiers, and women might become porters. Porters were people who carried supplies for the soldiers. My grandma was forced to be a porter from when she was thirty-two years old until she was about forty. It was a very dark time in her life, and she talked about villages that were burned. When my grandma was about forty and I was seven, our whole family moved to Thailand.

I had new life experiences at the camp. I met people from different ethnic groups like Thai and Burmese. And I met different religious people like Christians, Catholics, Buddhists, and Muslims. At the camp there were churches and temples. I used to go to the church. There were also schools, primary through high school, and even a college. At seven years old, I started going to school for the first time in my life. Actually, I was the first person in my whole family to ever go to school. That made me scared to start school.

My life in the refugee camp was a little better, but it still had many problems. Money and work were still big problems. We could not go out of the camp to find work, but we had to find a way to pay for things. The school was not free. You had to pay money for the education. If you didn't have money, you couldn't go to school. Some of the children had to stay at home and work because their parents didn't have money to support them. I had to walk to school because we didn't have school buses. Most people could not pay for electricity. When I studied for a test at night, I would use a candle. Finally, food was a big problem. There was not enough. Some foods, like beef, were really expensive. Some days I wouldn't have breakfast. Sometimes I would ask my mom for money to buy lunch. She gave me five baht, but it wasn't enough to buy anything. Some days I wouldn't have lunch either.

Even though we had problems, I felt lucky. My parents supported my school. We were able to pay the school fees because my parents sold vegetables they grew in a garden next to the house. On the days when we had food, I would eat vegetables mixed with fish paste and chili peppers for breakfast.

At eighteen, I was still living in the camp, and there were a couple of important people in my life. One person was my good friend Cherry Aye. We would hang out and go shopping for clothes or food. Sometimes we talked about family problems and going to America. My friend wanted to go to America, but she didn't have the UN photo like me. Another important person was a camp leader. One night he convinced my family to go to America. He told my parents, "If you want to move to the US, you can. And you don't need to pay money." When my parents heard that, they were so excited, and they applied for my family to go. This meant I was going to be reunited with my stepsister in America.

I had a stepsister living in Saint Paul for nine years. When we were young, she used to live with me in Thailand. But after she left, we just talked on the phone. She told me, "Ner may hen pen E nay, ner k' nay ba takuba-kuthay gaygay," which means, "If you come here, you are going to get a good education." This made me feel better about moving to America. In February 2016, I went to America. I flew on an airplane for about two days. On the plane I asked a woman, "Where is the toilet?" I wish I would have said the word "bathroom," but at the time I didn't know it. I had to stay in Japan for a while and then continue my journey to America. I didn't like the food on the airplane. When I finally arrived at the Minneapolis airport, my stepsister saw me first. I was excited We hugged and took a picture together.

The US was new to me. I met new people from different ethnic groups, just like when I first moved to the refugee camp. Now I was meeting Spanish, Mexican, and Somali people. When I first came here, I thought Mexican and American people looked the same. But now I know that they are different.

My life here in Minnesota has had hard moments and happy moments. At first, we didn't have transportation. So other Karen people in the community would give us rides. We would call them and sometimes we would give them twenty dollars to take us somewhere. We also didn't know how to speak English. That was hard for us. So sometimes I would talk to myself, I would tell myself, "Oh Kler, if you cannot speak English, what can you do? You have to try . . . for the future . . . you have to work. That's why you have to speak." I have also had some happy moments in Minnesota. I was happy when I started to go to LEAP High School. I met other Karen people there, and they helped me translate English I didn't understand. Even though life in America was new, my life was better than before.

Our whole family is making a new life here in Minnesota. My father has a job cleaning out the trash, and my mother takes care of our family. On weekends, we go to church together, visit my stepsister, or go to the park. And once, we went to the movie theater together. We didn't have movie theaters in the camp. Sometimes we go to a restaurant. We didn't have those in the camp either. We do laundry in a washing machine, not by hand like before.

At this time, I am twenty years old, and I'm making plans for the future. I want to be a chef. I like to make a Karen dish called biba—sticky rice with banana. I can also cook vegetables with meat. My dad, two brothers, and two sisters eat my food, but my mom doesn't like it. My mom thinks her cooking is better than mine. I'd also like to drive. Right now my stepsister drives me. I'm scared to drive. But I think that if I don't drive, nobody will keep driving for me.

There are still lots of people in Burma who want to come here, but they don't have UN photos. My friend still lives in the camp. We talk on Face-book. She doesn't have the UN photo; neither does my aunt or my grandma. My mom talks to her mom on the phone. Will they come? Could they come?

VIDEO LINKS

greencardvoices.org/speakers/oh-kler

Hla Yu Htoo

From: Tak, Thailand (Karen)
Current City: St. Paul, MN

"SPEAKING WAS REALLY DIFFICULT, AND I FELT REALLY SAD BECAUSE I DID NOT KNOW ENGLISH. SOMETIMES I WENT TO THE BATHROOM AND CRIED A LITTLE BIT, BUT I DIDN'T GIVE UP."

My name is Hla Yu Htoo. I am Karen, and I'm from Thailand. I lived with my family in the Mae La Camp. We didn't have enough food to eat, so I went to the forest with my dad to hunt animals, like mice, squirrels, birds, monkeys, or sometimes snakes. The snakes were dangerous, but we used to eat them. Also, we found vegetables to eat in the forest, like bamboo, ferns, mushrooms, and dogfruit. Sometimes there was fruit there. The fruit in the jungle tasted delicious, not like the food in the village.

I remember my parents working hard on the farm in Thailand. They had to work hard for our family. I always asked them for money to play marbles with my friends. One day, I wanted to know where the money came from. I asked my mom, but she didn't answer me. Then I saw my dad and said, "Dad, where does the money come from?" He said, "If you want to know where the money comes from, tomorrow you have to go with me to the farm." So, in the morning I went with him. On the way, the sun was very hot and I couldn't walk to the farm without taking a break. When I got there, I knew that my parents had to prove themselves and work hard for us. I knew that it is really hard to earn money, so I didn't ask for money anymore. We didn't have much, but we had enough money for food, clothing, and to enjoy life.

I didn't have any education, so my parents told me I had to go live with my grandma. I lived with my grandma to study at a high school. I studied at Thai school for six years. They taught me how to talk, how to write, and how to read. Now I can speak and write in Thai. But I don't know how to write Karen. When I lived with my grandmother, she always took care of my life. Every morning, she woke up early to cook for me, to get me ready, and to get me to school. She planned for my future. Maybe one day I might have a chance to have a better life to study higher education in the future. Education is the most important thing in my life.

My parents planned to come to the United States, but I didn't know about their plans. We had cousins in Minnesota. They sent a message to us to come here. They said that everything here is better than in Thailand; there is enough food here. When my parents heard that, they told me we planned to come here to have a better life. Where we lived in Thailand, you would work one day and earn money, buy things, and then the money would be gone. We planned to come to the US to have a better life and education, see different people and places, and plan for the future.

My mom and my dad had a party to say goodbye to my friends, my grandma, and some people in our neighborhood. When I saw my grandma, she was crying. I wanted to stay in the car, but I got out of the car, hugged my grandma, kissed her, and said, "I love you, my Grandma." I couldn't control my tears.

After that, we went to Mae Sot to check to see if we were healthy. After that, we went to Bangkok. The UN gave us money for the United States, gave us food, and took very good care of us. After that, we flew to Japan and then New York. We slept in New York one night. After that, I moved to Minnesota. It took three airplanes to get here.

I have cousins in St. Paul. When I got to the airport I saw them waiting for us; I was happy to see them. When we were in the airports, we didn't like to eat the food; it made my eyes swell and my skin scaly. We were skinny in the face, very dark. My cousins brought some Karen food to eat. I tasted it and felt better. My first time seeing snow, I was so surprised. It was amazing. I'd never seen snow before. I feel like I am on the Earth in the sky. I am so proud to be here.

My first time going to school was difficult. When I first went to school I had no friends, only my sister, but I didn't have the same class with her. In English, I just knew how to say yes or no. If my teacher asked me how I was, I didn't understand. I felt like I was learning like a kindergartner. Speaking was really difficult, and I felt really sad because I did not know English. Sometimes I went to the bathroom and cried a little bit, but I didn't give up. I told myself, "Don't give up. If you give up, it won't be good for you." I persevered to prove to myself I could learn English, so one day I will have a better future. I wanted to make my parents and my grandma in the refugee camp proud of me, so I tried my best.

I have been in the US three or four years. At first, it was difficult to live in St. Paul. We lived in an apartment building where there were black people and white people and no Karen. I was scared of black people and white people. I was scared they would fight me or tell the police to put me in jail, but they were so nice to us. After six months, my parents moved us to a new apartment in St. Paul. After two years, I knew how to speak English.

My life here is great. The food, education, and opportunities are better than my home country, and I have a car to drive. Right now, I am a senior. After I graduate, I plan to go to Saint Paul College and join the Army because I want to help our country.

VIDEO LINKS

greencardvoices.org/speakers/hla-yu-htoo

Vientiane,
Laos

Iya Xiong

From: Vientiane, Laos (Hmong)
Current City: St. Paul, MN

> "I CAN HELP MYSELF MORE THAN I COULD HELP MYSELF WHEN I LIVED IN LAOS. I FEEL PROUD BECAUSE I CAN EARN SOME MONEY BY MYSELF."

I was born in a small village. I was the third child and the youngest at the time. In 1999, when I was three years old, we moved to a suburb that was close to the city. We lived with my uncle because my dad was in France for the first time.

Then my dad came back after three months and we bought a house. We moved to live by ourselves. There were a lot Hmong people who lived in the community.

My dad went to France again for a second time while my mom was pregnant. This time my dad only lived in France for one month. Then, he flew over to the United States. My uncle, who is my dad's older brother, came first to the United States, and he lives in Minneapolis. They tried to apply for a visa, and he waited in the United States for four years, but he did not get any information, so he decided to come back in 2005. When he came back, we built a new house and my dad became a farmer.

While my dad was in France and in the United States, I spent my early childhood with my mom and three sisters. My mom bought a clothing store at the main market of the village. Life was very simple. Every day, after I woke up, I helped take care of my younger sister. My two older sisters helped each other prepare breakfast. My mom went to open the store. I started to go to school when I was six.

Seven years later, in 2012, someone contacted us and said that we could have our interview. But when we went there for the interview, we didn't pass because my dad had overstayed his visa. So we couldn't get into the country within ten years of that, so we had to wait until 2015 to get a second interview.

The second time I was not so excited because I knew that this time we were maybe going to pass the interview. When we passed the interview, I am not sure what my feeling was, but I think I was happy and also sad at the same time because I was going to leave everything behind. I was excited to see my sister because my two older sisters were already married and came to the US before us with their husbands. So I was excited to see them and to see my nieces and nephews, too.

Most of my cousins live here. That's why my father wanted to come to Saint Paul. He also wanted us to have a better life, too. I was excited when we got there. The airport was very big and my cousin came to wait for us. I was excited to see the country and how it looked. I was very excited.

We got our visa at the embassy. My parents did not let me go to school anymore, because I just finished high school and they did not want me to start college in Laos. We stayed home for a month before we flew over to the United States. We had to stop by different countries. We flew from Laos to Thailand and then to China. We got to Los Angeles first, and we stopped there to apply for our green card. We spent three hours there, and then we connected to fly to Minneapolis.

When we got here, it was morning and it was lightly snowing. It did not look like how I expected because all the ground was white and the trees looked dead. I was excited to see the snow. We lived in Minneapolis with my uncle first, but after a week I moved to Saint Paul to be able to go to LEAP High School. So I lived with my sister and her family in Saint Paul by myself.

Then I went to school at LEAP. The teacher was very nice and very helpful. First I was very nervous because I only knew easy words. I used to study in Laos, too, so that helped me a little bit. Then after a week, I saw some Hmong people, who lived in the same village with me in Laos. They helped me out sometimes and we also have some Hmong teachers that helped me out sometimes, too.

Everything is different from my country. In school, the grade levels are in different buildings, but here all the classes and levels are in the same building, and the way they teach here is different from my home country too. I feel like the way we learn here is easier than how I learned in Laos. The class size is also very different; in Laos we had forty-five to seventy students in class, and here we only have twenty-eight in the biggest class. We didn't have school buses, and school did not provide lunch.

For the first month, I didn't go to shopping. I just went to school and came home because my dad didn't have a car yet. After that, we bought a car, and then my sisters took me shopping for the first time after a month. The mall was very clean. We got to go shopping inside, not outside like in my country, and that was really nice.

My parents and my siblings still live with my uncle in Minneapolis. I didn't get to see my siblings and my parents for two weeks. They came to Saint Paul to visit me, and I was crying. Fortunately, they got hired by a company that is closer to Saint Paul than to Minneapolis, and they quickly rented a house and moved to Saint Paul. The house we live in here is smaller than the one in Laos.

I have been here for almost two years, and now I know how to drive. I also went to work during the summer. My job is packing up things. I can help myself more than I could help myself when I lived in Laos. I feel proud because I can earn some money by myself.

I can also help my family sometimes to take my mom to the store because she knows how to drive but she is not driving a lot. I help by reading letters and teaching them how to pay for the bills. Because I am the oldest child in the family, I help a lot. My parents don't know how to speak English, and that's why I help translate.

In my free time, I like to watch funny TV shows and listen to music. Sometimes, I try to contact my friends in Laos. It's hard because of the time difference.

My dad wants me to become a nurse, but I'm not sure if I can be a nurse. I would like to become a banker. I also really like to travel. Maybe I will travel back to my home country.

VIDEO LINKS

greencardvoices.org/speakers/iya-xiong

Morelos,
Mexico

Nelly Beltran-Espitia

From: Morelos, Mexico
Current City: Richfield, MN

"I'M THE FIRST PERSON IN MY FAMILY WHO WILL GRADUATE FROM HIGH SCHOOL AND GO TO COLLEGE, SO I FEEL VERY PROUD OF MYSELF."

My name is Nelly Berenice Beltran-Espitia. I am from Morelos, Mexico. I am twenty years old. I have been in the United States for five years.

When I was fifteen years old, I came to St. Paul, Minnesota, for the first time with my father. When we came, my father bought the airplane tickets. We arrived in Mexico City, and then from Mexico City to Chicago, and Chicago to here. I was so excited because I had never been in an airplane. Outside the weather was cold for me, because it was February, and it was winter time. My father, he didn't tell me that I had to bring a jacket or anything for cold weather. When I saw outside, it looked so ugly because everything looked sad. The trees without color, you know. We came and we took the taxi. We went to his apartment. I had one sister—who is older than me— living here with him, and I met her. Well, I knew her, but I hadn't seen her for like five to eight years, because my dad came here before, too. I saw her and I was so, so happy to see my sister. I stayed with them. I stayed with my family for like one month and then I started going to school. After one year, I started working.

I was in ninth grade when I came here. I started going to LEAP High School in St. Paul, Minnesota. There are many other Spanish speakers at my school, so I was able to speak Spanish when I needed to. There are also some teachers who speak Spanish there, too. I have been going to LEAP High School for four years. My English has changed so much since I started at LEAP. I can understand everything the teachers are saying, and I feel better about my life now than when I first came to the United States.

I am so happy to have found this school. LEAP has been for me a family. The staff always helps students and never leaves anyone alone. All teachers are wonderful and friendly. Also, they always smile and say hi to everyone. What should I say about my friends? They are amazing and friend-ly. I'm so happy with them because every time that I've needed help, they've helped me a lot. My favorite thing in my school is the Culture Party that is done every year. It is where we can express and show our culture. I'm glad for all my teachers, the social worker, the principal, and counselors for helping me a lot. LEAP is a small school, but we all respect each other and we help each other.

After one year, I started working and going to school at the same time. I started working at McDonald's. I worked five or six days a week. It just depended. I needed to help my father and my daughter. I have a daughter that had to stay back in Mexico. I need to send money back to help my mother raise her.

My first day at school was hard for me because I didn't speak any English at all. I thought I was going to quit school because it's hard. And my father told me, "No, you have to study because education is the most import-ant thing." My father told me, "You wanna clean toilets for your whole life? You wanna earn little money?" And I said, "No." That's why I am still going to school.

I'm in grade twelve. This is my last year. I will graduate this June with my high school diploma. Now I'm taking the hard classes, and I'm taking a CNA class, too. I want to be a nurse. Before I used to live here in St. Paul, but now I live in Richfield with my husband. I just had a beautiful baby girl. She is one month old. Her name is Ella.

In the future, I'm going to go to college to be a nurse or an aestheti-cian or a hairstylist. I am not sure which one I should choose. I know that I am going to go back to Mexico and bring my daughter back here to Minne-sota with me soon.

When I was fifteen years old, I had a baby. After I had my baby, she was like five months old and my father told me that we had my appointment in Ciudad Juarez, Chihuahua. He went back to Mexico, and he went with me to my appointment with immigration. We stayed in Chihuahua for two weeks. I had a lot of tests, like blood tests, and a lot of other things. When I had my appointment with immigration, they told me "Welcome to the Unit-ed States!" and I was so nervous and at the same time happy because I got my green card. We went back to Morelos, Mexico. After four months, my father bought an airplane ticket so I could come. My baby was eight months old when I came and I left her. Her name is Camila. She stayed back in Mexico and my mother has been raising her since I left for the United States. I know that to give my daughter a better life, I have to work hard now so I can get her to move up here with my husband, my newborn baby, and me. I want my family to be complete. I miss her every day. I cry when I think about her.

I see my daughter in the summers. Every summer, I go back to Mexico to visit my mom and my daughter and the rest of my family. I spend around two months there with my daughter. Now, she is five years old. She is a beautiful, smart little girl. Every time I talk to her or see pictures of her, I feel very emotional. I love her so much.

My life has changed so much over the last five years. I feel like the happiest woman in the world. Both of my daughters are the most important thing for me. Now I have to think more and be stronger than before. I feel a little bit sad because I have to go back to school and I don't want to leave my daughter, but I have to be strong. So I can get my high school diploma. After my graduation, my plan is to go back to my country and bring my daughter back here with me. I want to go to college because I want to be a hairstylist.

I'm the first person in my family who will graduate from high school and go to college, so I feel very proud of myself. I want my future to be next to my two princesses, my husband, and my mother.

VIDEO LINKS

greencardvoices.org/speakers/nelly-beltran-espitia

Wah Soe

From: Tak, Thailand (Karen)
Current City: St. Paul, MN

"I WANT TO BUILD A KAREN RADIO STATION, TOO. I HAVE A DREAM TO BE IN POLITICS AND I WANT TO GO HELP KAREN PEOPLE IN THE REFUGEE CAMP."

My name is Wah Soe. I was born in Thailand, and I grew up there. My family is from Myanmar. The Burmese people don't like Karen people, and they want to kill all Karen people and burn their homes. I was a student there at Nu Poe Camp. I lived there with my parents and my one brother. I went to school every day. My brother, Gabluh Soe, is twenty-three and married and lives in Minnesota now and has two kids. I live with my parents. My dad works at night and my mom stays at home and watches my nephew and niece.

At the camp, we didn't have enough opportunity for education. I lived there for fifteen years, but I never became a Thai citizen. We lived in a small camp and we couldn't leave. If we went out of the refugee camp, they'd catch us and put us in the jail. I raced animals, like pigs and chickens, to make my own money. It was serious. We had no money there so it was a way to get money. My father was a businessman, selling the diamonds from Myanmar and a cameraman. He was a leader in the community. I had a lot of friends there, but life in refugee camp was really hard.

Then I left camp to come here. The first day, I had to plan for the interview; on the second day, I had to get a shot; and the third, if you pass, you can come here. In 2012, I met at the UNHCR and they accepted my family into the US. I felt excited because we could get out of the refugee camp. Before we came here, I prayed to the God a lot, to come here. I was really sick, and the disease didn't disappear, so I asked God to help me and send me here. I thought we had a good possibility of being accepted into the US because in the refugee camp we didn't have human rights or good opportunities for education. I was so proud when they accepted me. The first time when I came out of the refugee camp and into the city, I looked at the tall buildings and said wow. I had never seen them before. It was really exciting to see the tall buildings. I freaked out.

In the plane, it took three days to come to the United States. I didn't have any relatives in St. Paul. I had to make new friends and a new community and learn about a new country. I was really depressed when I came here because I spoke zero English. I had to meet new friends and be part of a new community and learn about a new country.

I came here in October and started LEAP, but many didn't speak my language, Karen. There's totally a difference, and every day challenges me. The first time I came here to St. Paul, I was really cold and really depressed. But I had a beautiful teacher at the LEAP school. The teachers are really generous and supported me and gave me encouragement. I try hard, and I will get to my destination and what I am hoping for. I really appreciated the teachers at LEAP high school.

Snow is another difference. The weather is really cold here; where I lived, the weather was so hot. When I came here, I had to participate with different communities. Every day is totally different for me. My life is better here. In this country, we have equal rights.

I really appreciate my parents because they brought me to the United States, and they want me to go to school every day, and they support me. They kept an open mind for me, and they wanted me to go to school every day. Every day, they go to work and support me.

I participate in youth leadership at LEAP High School. I feel more comfortable now. I feel strong and energetic, better than before I came here. I made a lot of friends in my school, and I also participate in drama club. I also help the new students that come to LEAP High School.

Right now I'm a senior, and I will probably graduate this year in 2017. After I graduate, I want to learn more about politics. I also have a project I want to build called Openness in Miss Jiho's class at LEAP. I want to build a school for children that don't have parents, and to help the children in my country. Also a project called No Poverty and No More Hunger in Miss Amy's class. Right now we are working with poverty. We are researching the information, the negative impact and the positive impact. We researching India and Costa Rica. I want to build a Karen radio station, too. I have a dream to be in politics and I want to go help Karen people in the refugee camp. A lot still live there. I want to go to college and take political science and learn more about the community.

VIDEO LINKS

greencardvoices.org/speakers/wah-soe

Yangon,
Myanmar

Pare Meh

From: Yangon, Myanmar (Karenni)
Current City: St. Paul, MN

"I DIDN'T WANT TO MOVE. MY DREAM WAS TO BUILD MY LITTLE FAMILY WHERE I GREW UP. I THOUGHT THAT IF I MOVED, I'D MISS EVERY LITTLE THING I DID AND THE MEMORIES THAT I'D BUILT WITH MY NEIGHBORS AND MY FRIENDS."

I was born in Burma, and my family moved to Thailand when I was one. I grew up in Thailand. I lived in a camp called Section Twenty. I went to school and spent a lot of time with my mom and aunts. My mom sold street food. She got up early every morning. I used to help her a lot. She sold Karenni tofu, papaya salads, noodles salads, banana cupcakes, fried bananas, and hotdogs. I usually got up earlier in the morning to help my aunt too. Sometimes, I went with her to buy food. But I usually didn't sleep at home. I usually slept over with my friends. My dad was a hunter, and I saw him once a month. People in my neighborhood called him an animal husbandry professional.

I made it to fifth grade before my family decided to move to America. It was my dad's idea. He said he wanted to move because he wanted us to be educated and to stay away from dangerous places. We went to shopping to buy some new clothes. We packed up all our things and got ready to leave. I didn't want to go, but couldn't decide anything. So I just followed them. My two older sisters, one brother, one younger sister, parents, and grandma came with us. I felt so depressed. Life in a small town village was restful and tranquil. A few exciting things happened in that small town. We had restaurants, a movie theater, and markets, and the town was minutes away if I went by car or motorcycle. I didn't want to move. My dream was to build my little family where I grew up. I thought that if I moved, I'd miss every little thing I did and the memories that I'd built with my neighbors and my friends.

My cousin moved to the United States first. She lived alone in Boston. My mom worried about her. We decided to go to Boston too. We lived there for one year. My first day of school in Boston, it was me and my sister. We started in the same school, and there were not many Karenni people there. There were only one or two families. We couldn't speak or understand English. Learning a language that you've never heard before is so hard, and I felt so stressed.

My dad got a job washing dishes. But he needed stomach surgery, so he wanted to take a break, but his manager wanted him to work. So we decided to move to North Carolina. He took a break for a while, and then he started working in North Carolina.

When we first moved to North Carolina, there were a lot of people. They decided to move. Some people moved away, and we decided to move too. We heard that in Minnesota there were a lot of Karenni people. My parents want to be with Karenni people, so we decide to move.

There are many differences between America and my country. Here, we use electricity to cook. The light we use is electric too. In my country, we just used a wood fire to cook and a candle for light. It was surprising. I was scared when I first arrived. After a while, I tried to be calm and just start my life.

I liked living here for the last seven years. It's hard to believe that I've been here for that long because it feels like I left Thailand yesterday and I feel like I'm still brand new immigrant. I'll never forget the day I left. I am not sure if I will ever forget when I started longing to go back to my home country and never come back here again. But here I am. In the land of different colors of people. In a land that is currently enveloped in the "Trump Effect." I like living here, but I feel like I don't belong here any longer because of the new president. I'm so uncomfortable because of my skin color and where I'm from. I wish I was white so I could stay here and be happy here forever. I'm so sick of moving to another place to start my life over. I'm still thinking about my country, and I plan to go back some day.

It's fun here, and there are lots of things and opportunities. I get to do everything I want, and I can do whatever I want. My dad loves living here and he said he'll never go back to live in Thailand or in Burma.

My dream is to be a nurse. It's the only dream I've got. I plan to go to college if I can and reach my goal. I want to go to Century College because I heard that they have good ESL classes. I plan to go there for a year, and then I plan to transfer to Saint Paul College. I have been there twice, and I saw a lot of majors that I liked. There are classes for cooking, building houses, and fixing cars.

If I can be a nurse, I want to go back to my county and help sick people. I would also build a little hospital and a clinic so people can get treatment and live very long lives. Since I can speak English, I can teach the children English who don't go to school because they don't have money. I would like to stay there for many years and then come back to the US. I want to travel back and forth between the two countries. I want to build a house in Burma so that I can live here and there. I'd like a bamboo house because I used to sleep in a house like that. There will be a living room with a TV and sofa. Also, I want to open a business like a restaurant. I would sell noodle soup, like pho. I would sell a bowl of noodles for five dollars.

VIDEO LINKS

greencardvoices.org/speakers/pare-meh

Mogadishu, Somalia

Abshir Mohamed

From: Mogadishu, Somalia
Current City: St. Paul, MN

"I'D NEVER SEEN SNOW, AND I DIDN'T KNOW HOW IT WOULD LOOK LIKE. I THOUGHT HERE THAT THE FLOOR WOULD BE CLEAN LIKE GLASS. IT WASN'T LIKE HOW I IMAGINED."

I was born in Mogadishu, Somalia, at a hospital. I lived in a house with my big family. My aunties, my uncles, my mom, my grandma, and I lived there. When I was three years old, my mom left me with my grandma. When I was eight years old, my grandma died, and then my aunt took me in. She held onto me until we had to leave Mogadishu for somewhere safe.

My aunt works in a private school. She's an accountant, and she runs the buses too. They work with the school to pick students up and bring them to school, and I went to the same school she works at, starting from kindergarten. The school here is taught in English, and in Somalia most of them used to be taught in Arabic, but now it's changing. I went to the school called Al-Kowther Model School until grade nine. All the classes were taught in Arabic, except English. Most of the schools over there are part-time, from seven to twelve, so afterward I used to go Dugsi in Arabic, to learn the holy book, the Quran.

After a while living with my aunt, things got extreme like they had been in other cities in Somalia. We had to move to another city where we thought it was safer, but it wasn't. So we decided to move to Kenya because that was the only place we were sure there would be no violence going on like in Somalia.

We had no idea what we were going to do, and we were waiting to see if something was going to change. Then there were a lot of traveling vans trying to get through the border, and in that situation my aunt and I got divided. At the same time I heard that cargo trucks could sneak into Kenya, and could go through the border, so I thought I could go with them to get to Kenya. I hid in the back of a truck to get through, and it was actually hard to get in because the Kenyan government had put heavy security on the border.

I assumed that my aunt did the same thing. When I got to Kenya, I was young and all by myself, so it took me a long time to get adopted in the camps. I consider myself a lucky person to get through that kind of situation safely because some people would get cheated and sometimes got left behind. The worst part is that you can't hold those people responsible because they tell you before you leave that there will be dangers.

The name of the camp in Kenya is Ava, and it is the big camp there. I lived there a while trying to settle, until I decided to move to Nairobi, Kenya. I was told that some of my mother's friends lived there and that they could reach out to her. Later I found someone who could reach out to my mom, and that's how I got in touch with her. My mother told me that she was looking for me, then told me she would bring me to the United States. I don't remember when I got there, but I left in 2014. She sent me money to live with him, and he took care of me until I left from there. I came here by airplane in 2014.

My mom applied for a visa, and I had to wait for the process a long time. It took like two or three years. After I was accepted, it took a while for my visa to get to Kenya, so I waited down a long time. It also took a long time to get money to get the visa, so I didn't beg a lot. My mom told me, "You can have everything here, so just come here." She was waiting for me here, and I came here alone. I saw my mom for the first time. I didn't remember her when she left and I was expecting someone else, but I saw someone different when I got here.

Before I left, the only thing I was told was to get warm clothes. Kenya used to get snow. It was windy too, but I thought it would just be kinda cold when I got here. When I got here, it was freezing. It was not like Kenya. And I was like, "Wow." I'd never seen snow, and I didn't know how it would look like. I thought here that the floor would be clean like glass. It wasn't like how I imagined. My mom took me different places and introduced me to a lot of different people that she knew that are relatives here. I used to go with them all the time whenever they went somewhere. I was taken to different places, like malls.

I got here and went home, and I stayed two months before I started school because I didn't know English. Something got messed up and we applied for social security twice. We thought we had to have social security in order to go to school and later we found out that the school didn't need it and I could've just gone to school.

I didn't know anything. I was so shy at first. I came before the end of the school. I only stayed one month and a half in the school. I had the summer break and then I went back to school.

This year I actually don't have anything after school, but the last two years I used to be part of the YMCA program that did school activities, sports, and all that stuff. I didn't know English when I came, so I tried my best. I don't remember who told me, but I was told to ask questions. So I asked a lot of questions, and teachers loved that and that is what started to improve my English from that way to where I am right now, and I'm thankful for that.

It was hard for me to get in here, and I stayed after school to get help in English and math. This year I don't take math because of my schedule. I will take it next year.

I was planning to go to college after I graduate next year. I'm with the college basketball program, which is helping us through college for four years. I'll be senior next year. I want to try computer programming or anything to do with computers. There are a lot of topics, a lot of things to choose, so I haven't decided yet, but I want to get into that subject and that major.

Here it's so cold. I don't know if I will try to stay long here. I will work, and after I think I have got enough, I think I may move away to a different place, but not too far and not a place in particular.

VIDEO LINKS

greencardvoices.org/speakers/abshir-mohamed

Yu Mu Plaw,
Myanmar

Kzee Ya

From: Yu Mu Plaw, Myanmar (Karen)
Current City: St. Paul, MN

"I REMEMBER IT WAS REALLY HOT AND OUTSIDE LOOKED BEAUTIFUL AND THE TREES COLORFUL...IN MY COUNTRY, WE DON'T HAVE THE TREE COLORS LIKE THE UNITED STATES. WE HAVE TWO SEASONS THAT ARE RAINY AND SUNNY."

I was born in Burma, but I grew up in Thailand. My life was kind of difficult. When I lived in Thailand, we didn't have enough money for food and clothes. If we wanted to have clothes, we had to go find the work. We had to work hard, doing something like planting or being a farmer, and then we got the money.

I have two brothers and five sisters. I live with my parents. When I lived in Thailand, I helped my parents planting the plants, like banana trees, bamboo, mango trees, and pineapple trees.

When I was fourteen years old, I went to the place that I was born. It is called Yu Mu Plaw. I had to ride a boat to get to my aunts and uncles. They live at a place called Mae Nee Ta. In the morning we woke up and started to climb the tall hill to get into Yu Mu Plaw. When I got there, I saw my grandmother and grandfather. They are really old. I had never seen them. It was the first time meeting them. I was really happy. We shook hands with each other. My grandparents went to get me fruits that looked like blackberries. I went to the farm and picked up some vegetables near the river.

Before going to Thailand, we needed documents like a green card and citizenship, like in America. When I went to Thailand, I lived in the camps. I stayed in the camp the whole time. I never went out from the camp because when I went out of the camp, I was scared that the Thailand soldiers would catch me. When they catch you, they put you in jail. Some soldiers kill the people they catch. Some ask for money. If they ask for money, they will not take you to jail. If you have documents and show them, they leave you alone.

Before, my dad applied for us to go to a lot of different countries, but the other countries didn't take us. He said it was the last chance for him to apply to the United States and he got the answer. I told my dad I didn't

Kzee Ya

want move to the Unites States because I had a lot of friends, my old friends. I didn't want to come here, but I couldn't stay alone. We waited for eight months or something like that and then we left.

My family stayed in Mae Sot for one week, and then we traveled to Bangkok. Then we took an airplane to Korea, waited twenty minutes, and rode another airplane from Korea to New York. Then New York to Chicago, and Chicago to Minnesota.

When we got to Minnesota, our sponsor picked us up. We didn't know how to speak English. We just followed. The first day, I remember it was really hot and outside looked beautiful and the trees colorful. There are four seasons here. In my country, we don't have the tree colors like the United States. We have two seasons that are rainy and sunny. We have winter, but we do not have snow and it is not that cold. I just look outside and I cry and think about my old friends.

Here in the United States when we want to cook, we just have to turn on a knob to make fire. In Thailand, when we want to cook, we have to make fire with our hands. We need wood and ashes to make a fire. But in the United States, we just turn on the gas and it just comes on.

The first month I came here, one of my friends called me and said, "Can you go play volleyball in other states?" I went to Wisconsin to play volleyball. I have been playing since I was in fourth grade back in Thailand.

I went to eat the food in the Hmong Village. The food is similar to our old food when we lived in Thailand. There is pho and papaya salad. I remember the first time I flew in the airplane. I didn't eat anything; I just drank water. But now I can eat other things.

I think my life is better than before. When I lived in Thailand, we didn't have enough of certain things that we needed, like education, money, and food. But here in the United States, we have enough.

I will graduate this year. After I graduate, I will go to college. I want to become a kindergarten teacher. I would like to go to Saint Paul College. There is a program there called Child Development. I like to take care of the little babies. In my family, I am the oldest sister. In my future I want to become a teacher because I feel like I'm the one who always takes care of my little brother and the children. That is why I want to become a kindergarten teacher.

I like to write too. I like the writing class in high school. I received a certificate for best writer two times in my writing class.

Sometime, I go back to visit my mother because now I live with my cousin. My parents are living in another city. When we go there we just make a barbecue with my sister and brother. We cook pork, chicken wings, and crabs. We eat it together. It is so good.

Now my parents are living in Austin, Minnesota, because my mother works there. My mom works cutting the meat. My mother doesn't want to be living alone, but my dad bought a house there. They live together now. After I graduate, I will go visit my family in Austin. I want to stay here until I graduate. I want to stay here, and I want to go college.

This summer I will get married. I met him at church, but that time I didn't know that he liked me. One of my friends at school asked for my information so that he could give it to my boyfriend now. The first time when I met with him, I didn't want to be in a relationship. I still wanted to be single. After a few months, I went to visit him at his home. His family was so nice to me, so I started to like him. We have been dating almost four years. He asked me to marry him and I told him to wait until I am twenty-five years old, but I changed my mind because I don't want him to be with another person. We broke up once, and it was really hard on me.

When I get married, the family will prepare a big dinner. There will be pork, chicken, and vegetables. There will be a lot of people and friends to join us. They will come from different places. I will be wearing my Karen traditional clothing.

VIDEO LINKS

greencardvoices.org/speakers/kzee-ya

Mexico City,
Mexico

Javier Arreola Martell

From: Mexico City, Mexico
Current City: St. Paul, MN

> "I DECIDED TO COME SO THAT I COULD BUILD A BETTER FUTURE FOR ME AND MY FAMILY. THE BEGINNING WAS KIND OF HARD BECAUSE I DIDN'T SPEAK ENGLISH. I DIDN'T KNOW ANYONE."

I am from Mexico. When I was three years old, my parents got divorced. My father took me with my older brother to a state named Hidalgo, and I lived there with my grandma for almost my whole life. I met my mother when I turned six. After a few months, my father decided to go to the US, and I stayed with my grandmother and my older brother. When my brother graduated from middle school, my mother came to visit us. We both decided to go live with her. After a year, she decided to come to the US with my father, so she asked my aunt to take care of us. There were four of us: my older brother, two little brothers, and me. After that, I decided to go back and live with my grandmother. She mostly raised me. When I was fifteen years old, I decided to tell my father that I wanted to come live with him. So he bought my ticket and I came. It was really hard because I had to say goodbye to my grandmother and the rest of my family, whom I miss a lot right now. But I am happy to be here. I know that being here will help me build a better future for me and my family. That is the reason why I decided to come to the US.

My childhood was really hard. I did not have time to make a lot of friends because I was moving from state to state. But I think it was a good chance to learn about my family, my culture, and also some different languages that people were still speaking in those states. At the same time, it was kind of hard because I didn't have a lot of friends. I am a shy person. It is hard for me to talk with new people.

When my grandma was coming home from work, my older brother and I used to wait for her because she always brought something for us, like candy or toys. That made me happy. I really love my grandma. She always knew how to make us happy, even in those hard times. She gave us the love that our parents didn't give us.

113

Before I came to the US, I used to play soccer in school. On my weekends, I used to practice parkour with my older brother and our friends. It was just such a wonderful experience. That helped me a lot at the school and also making new friends.

I flew from Mexico City to Atlanta, Georgia. My mother and my uncle were waiting for me at the airport. I didn't speak English, so I didn't know where to go. I was lost, so I asked one of the security guards for help, and they called the interpreter. He helped me find my mother and uncle. Then she took me to where she was living. I stayed with her for two weeks, and then I met my father. He came to Atlanta to pick me up, and then we came to Minnesota. I hadn't seen my mother for five years and my father for eleven years. It was hard, and still is hard, because I didn't remember a lot of how they were when I was a kid. It was hard being with my father at the beginning because he didn't raise me, and same with my mother. I know that they are my parents and I love them both, but in this case I will say that my grandmother is like both of my parents. My grandmother taught me what my parents didn't.

I decided to come so that I could build a better future for me and my family. The beginning was kind of hard because I didn't speak English. I didn't know anyone. It was hard to socialize with my classmates because I didn't speak English. But it was good somehow because there were people that helped me on my first day of school. They translated things that my teachers told me. They took me to my classes, and they were very nice with me. But still, it was hard because even now that I speak English, I feel like I am different from other people just because I am from a different country and I speak a different language. But I am happy to be here with my family which is most important for me.

The US is such a beautiful place. American people are very nice. The places here are wonderful. It's kind of different from my country but not that much. It's still an interesting place for me. I wanted to see it with my own eyes because I used to watch movies when I was a kid. But it is not the same feeling when you come here and see everything with your own eyes.

It was hard in the beginning because I didn't speak English and I didn't know the places and things like that. But my father helped me somehow. He helped me a lot in school and at home. I made new friends and they helped me to survive through school and here in this country.

My life now has changed in a good way. I'll graduate from high school pretty soon. My English has improved. I have lots of friends. I am happy. I am happy thanks to those people that are around me, my teachers, my classmates, and my family.

What I like to do on my free time and especially during summer is to practice parkour. I also do some exercise. I don't like to read; I do read sometimes but not very often. I also play video games. I hang out with my friends on weekends at different places like Minnehaha Falls and Mounts Park. I like those two places. I find them very peaceful.

I used to work in a Mexican supermarket, but I quit a few months ago. I worked for about one year there, and it was a good experience. I quit because I got bored of doing the same thing each day.

Last summer break, I went to visit my mother. She is living with my little sister, who is three years old. I also visited my uncle, who is living close to where mother lives. I stayed there for about a month, and I loved it. I had a lot of fun with my mother and sister.

I am gonna stay here in this country with my father and my thirteen-year-old sister. After I graduate from high school, I want to go to college and become a scientist. After that, I'll be a teacher and go back to my country so I can help my people—but not just my country. I also want to help other countries.

VIDEO LINKS

greencardvoices.org/speakers/javier-arreola-martell

Tak,
Thailand

Ma Ka Lah

From: Tak, Thailand (Karen)
Current City: St. Paul, MN

"MY GOAL IS TO BECOME A NURSE. THEN I COULD HELP SICK PEOPLE AND HELP TREAT PATIENTS. RIGHT NOW I AM ALREADY THE CAREGIVER FOR MY GRANDPA."

Gaw ler gay—good morning! My name is Ma Ka Lah and this story is about my life from the time I was born until now. I was born in a refugee camp located in Thailand near the Myanmar and Thailand border called Mae La. When I was little, I lived there with my grandparents because my parents left us to find money in another place to live. So I lived with my grandparents, and I had to help them. I had to cook in the morning, help wash the clothes, and take care of my younger brothers and sister.

When I was not at home helping out, I had to go to school. The school building was a small room; the roof was made of leaves, and the floor was made of bamboo. If you go to school in Thailand, you have to wear a uniform. The shirt is white and the skirt is dark blue.

The only problem with school was I didn't like it. I always skipped a couple of days of school each week. But one day my teacher told my grandparents about what I was doing, and my grandparents yelled at me. They wanted me to go to school. So I tried to go to school more. For me, school was kinda boring and hard. I didn't like to learn. If we failed a test, our teacher would hit us with a stick. She might hit our hands, legs, or butt. Or sometimes she would make you stand up and sit down again and again. That's why I didn't want to go to school.

Then one day I learned a new idea, but I didn't learn about it at school. I was thirteen years old and my parents had come back to the camp because my mother was pregnant with my youngest brother. My mom and my dad talked about the idea of going to America. Until that day, I had never thought about going to the United States. But I kept that idea in my mind, and I continued living in the camp for about another eight years. Sometimes, thinking about the United States made me scared. I heard some people say

117

that in the United States, white people eat humans. But my eldest sister who had already arrived in the United States said, "Come here!" And, she told me that this was not true—that the white guys eat people. Since I didn't want to live in the camp anymore, I decided to go to the United States. My sister had already gone, and now my plan was to go with my grandparents. I wanted to learn more.

The time had come to leave the camp. A big bus, as big as a school bus, came to pick us up along with the other refugee people. We had to leave early in the morning, like six a.m. We got on the bus and went to a place called Maesod. When we got over there, they checked our physical health to see if we were sick or not. They gave each person a jacket and one pair of shoes. Before I left, they gave me breakfast too. After that, I got on a bus to Bangkok, and stayed for one night. They gave me dinner, and in the morning they gave me breakfast too. After we ate breakfast, we went to the airport to get on the airplane. We waited there for so long. A person helped us by showing us how to get the ticket and how to get the passport picture. We didn't have passports until that day; before that we only had pictures of ourselves with a logo of the United Nations. With the last of the paperwork done, we were helped onto the airplane. After we got on the airplane, I flew from Thailand to China to New York. When we arrived in New York, it was around nine p.m. We had to stay over one night. They gave me dinner. In the morning, people helped us wake up. They gave me breakfast, and then they took me to the airport again. This time we flew from Chicago to Minneapolis. In the United States, people also helped us. They showed me how to get on the airplane and transfer.

Finally, I arrived in Minneapolis. Now, I had to find my luggage. I tried to ask someone, "Where is the luggage?" But then my sister saw me because she recognized my grandparents. We didn't recognize each other because it had been such a long time. We were both so excited to see each other again. So my sister's friends and my caseworker took me at home. I was tired. And, by the way, I didn't like the food that they gave me on the airplane.

Now it was time to face my first days and weeks in America. In my first days, I had to go to the lab clinic to get a shot and my blood checked. This was a lab check for diseases, but I didn't have any. Before I could go to school I had to get another shot, in addition to getting my eyes and my ears checked. Now I could go to school. My caseworker helped me register.

In the following weeks, I found that Minnesota was very different from my home. It's different because in Minnesota the houses are made of bricks, and there are many roads and cars. I had never seen apartments and tall buildings; now we rented a room in one of the tall buildings. In Thailand, the house we lived in was made by my grandparents. The roof was made with leaves and the floor was made of bamboo. The restroom was built away from the house with the same materials. So Minnesota felt different to me.

School in the United States was also different. The first day when I went to school, I felt very excited and nervous because I didn't know how to speak English. But I made some friends at the school who were Karen, and they tried to help me. They told me how to get to class, and they explained things to me. When the teacher was teaching in English, I only understood a little bit. The subjects I liked the most were math and science. I didn't like writing and reading because they were hard for me. Writing is trying to think a lot; you have to make your own ideas. Because I am not good at English, I didn't like it.

So that is my life up until now. I also have some plans for the future about college and a career. I might study abroad. I would like to study more about science, math, psychology, and nursing. My goal is to become a nurse. Then I could help sick people and help treat patients. Right now I am already the caregiver for my grandpa. My grandma passed away last fall. But by caring for them, I know that I want to help other people too. This is one of the reasons I know I want to be a nurse.

On one further personal note, in the future I would also like to see my parents again. They are living in the camp still. We talk on Facebook, but I miss them and I hope I will be able to visit them again. And that concludes the story of me.

VIDEO LINKS

greencardvoices.org/speakers/ma-ka-lah

Papu,
Myanmar

Lu Lue

From: Papu, Myanmar (Karen)
Current City: St. Paul, MN

"IN GYM CLASS, WHEN THE TEACHER ASKED US TO PICK A PARTNER TO PLAY BASKETBALL, I HAD TO SIT AND WATCH KIDS PLAY BECAUSE I DIDN'T KNOW ANYBODY AND I DIDN'T KNOW ANY ENGLISH. I JUST HAD TO SIT AND WATCH."

I was born in Myanmar. When I was two years old, my parents moved to Thailand because of the Myanmar soldiers. They burned down the houses in my village. So we ran away from our village to live in a refugee camp in Thailand.

During our move to Thailand, we had to sleep in the forest to hide from the soldiers. I almost lost my life at that time. My dad put me on his shoulders for a long time. When he put me down, my legs were numb and I couldn't walk. I fell down the hill and was knocked unconscious.

When we got to Thailand, we had to stay in the camp, and there were no jobs. We couldn't go out looking for jobs. If you went out, if the Thai police saw you, they would catch you, and they'd put you in jail. So we had to stay in the camp and eat what they gave us. The UNHCR gave us rice, red chili peppers, fish paste, cooking oil, and other things.

In the camp, I went to school and took care of my brothers and sisters. There was no playground and no grass. You had to stay home and play with friends on the dirt. We played rock games and rubber band games on the ground, so we got dirty. Sometimes we got sick from it.

In Thailand, I had many jobs to do. My dad was far away because he had to look for jobs. Otherwise we'd have no money. So most of the time, I had to be in my dad's place. I had to go into the forest with my friends and look for food. In Thailand, we have deep forests. I got scared, but I had no choice; we had to go. Otherwise we would have no food to eat. The only things that I was afraid of were ghosts and getting lost. In Thailand, especially the place where we lived, a lot of dead soldiers were in those forests, and sometimes they'd haunt you. In addition, the forests are so deep that sometimes you can lose your way and keep circling. Those forests are very dan-

121

gerous, especially for kids. Another danger in the forest was the mosquitoes. When the mosquitoes bit you a lot, you got sick from it.

Sometimes I had to cross the river to look for bamboo and mushrooms. We used machetes to cut the bamboo and wood. Every Saturday and Sunday morning, I had to wake up early so that I could get flowers. We have big trees, and you can pick the flowers to sell when they fall on the ground.

I went to school in the refugee camp. We had to pay to go to school. As we went up in grade, we had to pay more money. It was hard to find money in a camp because we barely had jobs. My father gave me the money to pay for our school and some food. In our school, we had to wear a uniform. They separated boys and girls in the class. Girls had to sit on one side of the room and boys on the other side of the room. The teacher would punish us if we failed a test or if we didn't do our homework. They would hit us with a stick or make us run around the school.

When I came to America, we had to stop and change planes several times. On the plane the first time, I was very dizzy, and I didn't like the food. The pressure in my ears made it hard to hear. Also, I didn't know how to use the bathroom. The door was very different, and I got locked in. And the toilet was very weird to use. When we got off the plane, we got scared that we might get lost because we didn't know anything. We only knew words like "yes," "no," "up," and "down," and phrases like "What's your name?" and "I am from Thailand." It was so difficult for us to understand what people were saying. My parents were so worried that we might get lost. When we got to Chicago, one of the IOM members came to get us and took us to the hotel. We had to stay in a hotel for a night, and then we took another airplane to North Carolina. We didn't like any of the food they gave us at the hotel. I didn't like the smell. I didn't like anything when I first came. But I liked the bed. In Thailand, we slept on the floor.

Life in North Carolina was very hard. When I first started going to school, I was thirteen and I had no friends. I remember I had to sit in the cafeteria for a year alone. In gym class, when the teacher asked us to pick a partner to play basketball, I had to sit and watch kids play because I didn't know anybody and I didn't know any English. I just had to sit and watch. In class too, when the teacher said to pick a partner, I had no partner and had to work alone. The teachers weren't helping. They were on their laptops, sitting at their desks, doing their job—maybe. In North Carolina, I just went to school and took care of my brothers and sisters.

I lived in North Carolina for three years. After that we decided to move to Minnesota because we didn't have Medicare in North Carolina and there were not a lot of jobs. We had friends in Minnesota. They said they provided medical care, so we moved here. I like it here. We have more Karen people, and when you need help you can call someone. I was so excited that I got to see a lot of my old friends. I like to live here. But I don't like the weather.

In Minnesota I go to LEAP High School. In North Carolina, I went to West Millbrook Middle School. I didn't really know anybody in Millbrook, but at LEAP school I know all my classmates and they're nice. In LEAP, I have friends that are willing to help because they have been in LEAP for a long time. Right now I'm in twelfth grade and I like writing and social studies. And I also like basketball and soccer. On weekends I still watch my brothers and sisters, but sometimes I sing and play with them too. I'm hoping that in the future I'll become an art or social studies teacher. I like art and social studies because I'm so bad at math, and you don't have to do algebra or geometry in those two subjects. Math is not my subject.

I have four sisters and three brothers. My mom has to take care of my brothers and sisters, and my dad works far away—like two hours away. And he only comes back once a week. Sometimes he can't. Sometimes we have to worry about bills. And sometimes we are afraid that we might become homeless because the house bills are so high. My dad works so hard, but he gets low wages. Besides this, I'm happy. I like my school and I'm happy with my friends. But when I look at my family side, I'm kind of sad.

VIDEO LINKS

greencardvoices.org/speakers/lu-lue

Afterword

Learning from the students' stories in this book is just the beginning. The more important work starts when we engage in difficult but necessary conversations about the changing face of our nation.

Immigration plays a significant role in modern America; one in five Americans speak a language other than English at home. From classrooms to bookclubs, from the individual interested in learning more about his immigrant neighbor to the business owner looking to understand her employees and business partners, this book is an important resource for all Americans.

For these reasons, we have included a portion of our Act4Change study guide, a glossary, and links to the students' video narratives, intended to expand the impact of these students' journeys to the United States. The Act4Change study guide is an experiential learning tool. It promotes participation scaffolded with thoughtful discussion questions and activities that are designed for hands-on learning, emphasizing personal growth. It will help teachers, students, and all participants examine their own stories.

We hope to spark deeply meaningful conversations about identity, appreciation of difference, and our shared human experience.

If you would like an extended version of the study guide or to learn about educator workshops on how to use the Act4Change study guide, visit our website—*www.greencardvoices.org.*

Act4Change
A Green Card Voices Study Guide

Each person has the power to tell their own story in their own voice. The art of storytelling translates across cultures and over time. In order to learn about and appreciate voices other than our own, we must be exposed to and given tools to foster an understanding of a variety of voices. We must be able to view the world from others' perspectives in order to act as agents of change in today's world.

Green Card Youth Voices is comprised of the inspirational voices from a young group of recent immigrants to the US that can be shared with a wide audience. This study guide will provide readers with questions to help them explore universal themes, such as storytelling, immigration, identity, and perspective.

Introduce New Voices:

Participants will select one of the twenty-one storytellers featured in *Green Card Youth Voices* and adopt that person's story as his or her own "new voice." For example, one participant may choose Farhat Sadat while another might choose Mario. Participants will become familiar with the life story of their "new voice" and develop a personal connection to it. After each participant has chosen his or her "new voice," read the personal essay first and then watch the video.

Act4Change 1 :
Answer the following questions—
1. Why did you select the storyteller that you did?
2. What was interesting to you about his/her story?
3. What do you and the storyteller have in common?
4. What have you learned as a result of reading/listening to this person's story?

Learn About New Voices 1:

Divide participants into groups of three or four people. Provide each group with copies of the written narratives from five selected stories. Each person within each group will read one of the five narratives. Once finished, the participants will share their narratives with the others. Then, as a group, choose one of the five "voices" and watch that person's video.

Afterward, go on to the journal activity below.

Act4Change 2:
Answer the following questions—

1. What new information about immigrants did you learn from this second storyteller?
2. Compare and contrast the storyteller's video to his/her story. Which did you prefer? Why?
3. What are some similarities between you and the second storyteller?
4. If this really was your "new voice," what might you want to know about America upon arriving?
5. If you could only bring one suitcase on your move to another country, what would you pack in it? Why?

Learn About New Voices 2:

Each participant will be given a third "new voice," and only one can go to each student; there can be no duplicates.

Inform participants not to share the identity of their "new voice." Participants will try to match their classmates' "new voices" to one of the stories in the book. Encourage participants to familiarize themselves with all of the voices featured in *Green Card Youth Voices.*

Act4Change 3:

1. After they are given their "new voice," ask participants to try and create connections between this third voice and themselves. Have the students read their story and then watch the video of their "new voice." Have them think of a piece of art, dance, song, spokenword, comic, sculpture, or other medium of their choosing that best describes their "new voice."

2. Participants will present a 3-5 minute artistic expression for the larger group from the perspective of their "new voice" in thirty-five minutes. The audience will have a template with a chart that includes each of the thirty GCYV students' names, their photo, and a one- or two-sentence abbreviated biography. Audience members will use this chart throughout the activities to keep track of what has been learned about each voice that they have heard.

3. Ask the participants to describe the relationship between the Green Card Youth Voices and themselves:

    a. What did you notice about the form of artistic expression and the story?

    b. What drew you to this specific art form?

    c. Do you notice any cultural relationships between the "new voice" and the piece of art that was chosen?

    d. What is your best advice to immigrant students on how to succeed in this country? State? City?

More than Meets the Eye:

In small groups, have participants read and watch three or four selected narratives from *Green Card Youth Voices*. After that, have group members tell each other facts about themselves and tell the others in the group what they would not know just by looking at them. For example, participants can share an interesting talent, a unique piece of family history, or a special interest. Then have group members discuss things that they found surprising about the students in *Green Card Youth Voices*.

Think about the "new voice" you transformed in Act4Change 3. Tell your group something that was "more than meets the eye" from the perspective of that "new voice!"

For the complete version of *Act4Change: A Green Card Voices Study Guide*, visit our website—www.greencardvoices.org

See also:

Act4Change: A Green Card Youth Voices Study Guide, Workshop for Educators
This workshop is a focused learning experience crafted to deepen teacher understanding and provide instructional strategy, particularly designed to be used in conjunction with *Green Card Youth Voices*.

Glossary

Afrikaans: a language of southern Africa, derived from the form of Dutch brought to the Cape by Protestant settlers in the seventeenth century, and an official language of South Africa.

animal husbandry professional: a person who works with the care and breeding of different kinds of animals.

Baht: the currency of Thailand.

bamboo: a grassy plant with hollow stems common across Asia and also native to sub-Saharan Africa.

Bangkok: the capital and most heavily populated city of Thailand.

biba: sticky rice with banana.

Burma: a sovereign country in Southeast Asia officially known as the Republic of the Union of Myanmar. Burma is bordered by Bangladesh, Indian, China, Laos, and Thailand and home to over fifty-one million people.

Burmese: the official language of Myanmar (officially the Republic of the Union of Myanmar, and also known as Burma).

camp leader: a person who is chosen to lead their community in a refugee camp.

caregiver: a person who helps take care of another individual needing assistance due to illness, aging, or disability.

carne asada: thinly sliced grilled meat.

caseworker (also case manager): a person appointed to provide refugees with assistance upon acceptance into the country. They are in direct contact with refugees to assist them with daily necessities and legal immigration requirements. Caseworkers generally have a background in social work or counseling.

cataracts: a clouding of the eye lens that leads to decreased vision, including faded colors, blurry vision, and trouble seeing at night. Cataracts are most commonly due to aging but can occur after eye trauma or injury.

chaperone: a person who supervises young people during social occasions.

clubs: groups that play soccer/sports together.

cyber cafe: an internet cafe open to the public

defender: a soccer position with the job of winning back the ball from the opposing team and preventing them from scoring.

DV (Diversity Visa): The Diversity Immigrant Visa Program (DV Program) makes up to fifty thousand immigrant visas available annually, drawn from a random selection among all entries to individuals who are from countries with low rates of immigration to the United States. The DV Program is administered by the US Department of State (DOS). Commonly called the Green Card Lottery, it is a United States congressionally mandated lottery program for receiving a Lawful Permanent Resident Card (also referred to as a 'green card').

ESL/ELL/EL: English as a Second Language/English Language Learner/English Learner—all words to describe English language study programs for non-native speakers.

fish paste: fish which has been chemically broken down by a fermentation process until it reaches the consistency of a soft creamy paste, commonly used as seasoning.

gaw ler gay: 'Good morning' in Karen language

granadillas: an edible fruit in the passionflower family

Green Card Lottery: see "Diversity Visa Lottery" above.

green card: a commonly used name for a Lawful Permanent Resident Card, an identification card attesting to the permanent resident status of an immigrant in the United States. The green card serves as proof that its holder, a Lawful Permanent Resident (LPR), has been officially granted immigration benefits, which include permission to reside and take employment in the United States. Green card also refers to an immigration process of becoming a permanent resident.

Hmong: an ethnic group from the mountainous regions of China, Vietnam, Laos, Myanmar, and Thailand, thousands of whom resettled in Western countries following the aftermath of the Vietnam War and the Laotian Civil War.

immigration: the movement of people into a country other than their homeland where they do not possess citizenship, in order to settle, work, or live there as permanent residents, naturalized citizens, or foreign workers.

interpreter: a person who orally translates one language to another.

IOM: the International Organization for Migration.

Johannesburg: the largest city in South Africa and one of the fifty largest urban centers in the world.

Karen: An ethnic group comprised of approx. 5.5 million people that can be found in southern and southeastern Myanmar and Thailand. Also the language spoken by the Karen people.

Karenni: an ethnic group living primarily in Kayah State of Myanmar.

Karenni tofu: a Karenni food made from soybeans.

lab clinic: a medical clinic where people can have basic medical tests done.

Lisu: an ethnic group residing in northern Myanmar, Thailand, China, and northeast India.

Mae La: a refugee camp in Thailand established in 1985 that currently houses about fifty thousand Burmese refugees, over 90 percent of whom are ethnic Karen.

Mae Ra Moe: a refugee camp in Thailand

Mae Sot: a district in western Thailand that shares a border with Burma, or the Republic of Myanmar.

missionaries: a person sent to a particular area, like a refugee camp, to carry out a specific mission, often religious in nature.

oma & opa: grandmother and grandfather in Thai language

orientation (in refugee camps): education on the customs of the country in which a refugee will be resettled.

papaya salad: a spicy salad made from shredded unripe papaya and eaten throughout Southeast Asia.

pho: a Vietnamese noodle soup consisting of broth, rice noodles called bánh phở, a few herbs, and meat, primarily beef or chicken.

porter: a person hired to carry baggage.

poza de agua: Spanish phrase refering to a borehole well

primary school: lower elementary schools in South Africa, typically serving children for seven years until age fifteen.

refugee camp: temporary housing for people displaced by warfare or religious or political reasons.

refugee: a person who is outside their country of residence or nationality and is unable or unwilling to return to their original country of residence or nationality because of persecution or a well-founded fear of persecution on account of race, religion, nationality, membership in a particular social group, or political opinion.

social worker: a person who works in schools, hospitals, government agencies, or nonprofits and provides social services for individuals, especially those are are economically disadvantaged.

UN photo: a photo taken when refugees goes through the resettlement process

UNHCR (United Nations High Commissioner for Refugees): is a United Nations program that supports and protects refugees at the request of a government or the UN. In addition to providing critical emergency assistance in the form of clean water, sanitation and healthcare, the UNHCR assists refugees in resettlement or returning to their country of origin.

visa process: a nonimmigrant or immigrant application submitted to the US Embassy or Consulate to obtain an immigrant or nonimmigrant visa.

visa: a physical stamp in a passport, or document granted by a US Embassy or Consulate outside the US, that permits the recipient to approach the US border and request permission to enter the US in a particular immigrant or nonimmigrant status.

xenophobia: the fear and distrust of people or cultures that are perceived to be foreign or strange. Xenophobia is sometimes used interchangeably with racism because people who share a national origin may also belong to the same race.

Immigrant Youth Traveling Exhibits

Twenty students' stories from each city in the *Green Card Youth Voices* series (Minneapolis, Fargo, and St. Paul) are featured in traveling exhibits, available to schools, universities, libraries, and other venues where communities gather. Each exhibit features twenty stories from a particular city, each with a portrait, a 200-word biography, and a quote from each immigrant. A QR code is displayed next to each portrait and can be scanned with a mobile device to watch the digital stories. The following programming can be provided with the exhibit: panel discussions, presentations, and community-building events.

Green Card Voices currently has six exhibits based on different communities across the Midwest. To rent an exhibit, please contact us at 612.889.7635 or info@greencardvoices.org.

Green Card Youth Voices: Book Readings

Meeting the student authors in person creates a dynamic space in which to engage with these topics firsthand. Book readings are a wonderful opportunity to hear the students share their stories and answer questions about their lived experiences.

To schedule a book reading in your area, please contact us at 612.889.7635 or info@greencardvoices.org.

About Green Card Voices

Founded in 2013, Green Card Voices is a Minneapolis-based, nationally growing social enterprise that works to record and share first person narratives of America's immigrants to facilitate a better understanding between immigrant and non-immigrant communities. Our dynamic, multimedia platform, book collections, and traveling exhibits are designed to empower a variety of educational institutions, community groups, and individuals to acquire first-person perspectives about immigrants' lives, increasing the appreciation of the immigrant experience in America.

Green Card Voices was born from the idea that the broad narrative of current immigrants should be communicated in a way that is true to each immigrant's story. We seek to be a new lens for those in the immigration dialogue and to build a bridge between immigrants and nonimmigrants— newcomers and the receiving community—from across the country. We do this by sharing the firsthand immigration stories of foreign-born Americans, and by helping others to see the "wave of immigrants" as individuals with interesting stories of family, hard work, and cultural diversity.

To date, the Green Card Voices team has recorded the life stories of over three hundred immigrants coming from more than one hundred different countries. All immigrants who decide to share their story with GCV are asked six open-ended questions. In addition, they are asked to share personal photos of their life in their country of birth and in the US. The recorded narratives are edited down to five-minute videos filled with personal photographs, an intro, an outro, captions, and background music. These video stories are available on www.greencardvoices.org, and YouTube (free of charge and advertising).

Green Card Youth Voices: Immigration Stories from a St. Paul High School was the third book in the *Green Card Youth Voices* series. It was followed by *Immigration Stories from an Atlanta High School*. GCV has also published *Green Card Entrepreneur Voices: How-To Business Stories from Minnesota Immigrants*.

Contact information:
www.greencardvoices.org
info@greencardvoices.org • 612.889.7635

Facebook: www.facebook.com/GreenCardVoices
Twitter: www.twitter.com/GreenCardVoices

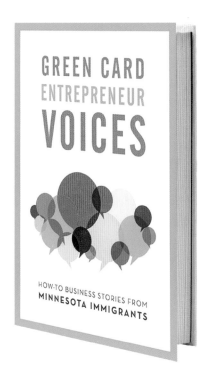

Also available:
Green Card Youth Voices:
Immigration Stories from an Atlanta High School

This book is a collection of twenty-one personal essays written by refugee and immigrant students, and one teacher from Cross Keys High School Clarkston High School and DeKalb International Student Center in Atlanta, Georgia. The young storytellers—including six DACA recipients—come from nineteen different countries and reveal in their own words the complexity and humanity of the immigration experience that is too often obscured in current conversations. Available as an ebook (ISBN: 978-1-949523-08-9) and paperback (ISBN : 978-1-949523-05-8).

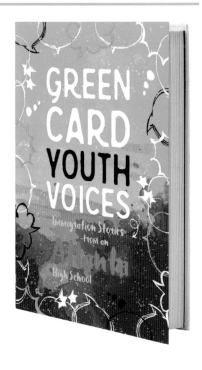

Contents:

- Full color portraits
- 21 personal essays by students from around the world
- Links to digital video stories on the Green Card Voices website
- Foreword by Luma Mufleh, Founder and CEO of Fugees Family, Inc. and Head Coach of the Fugees Soccer Teams
- Excerpt from *Act4Change: A Green Card Voices Study Guide*
- Glossary

To purchase online and view a list of retailers, visit greencardvoices.org/books.

Also available on Amazon.

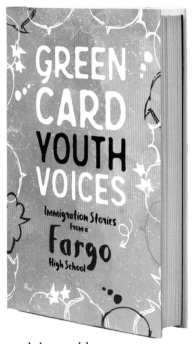

Green Card Youth Voices:

Immigration Stories from a Minneapolis High School

The first book in the Green Card Youth Voices series, *Green Card Youth Voices: Immigration Stories from a Minneapolis High School* is an unique book of personal essays written by twenty-nine students from Wellstone International High School. Coming from thirteen different countries, these young people share stories of family, school, change, and dreams. The broad range of experiences and the honesty with which these young people tell their stories is captured here with inspiring clarity. Available as an ebook (ISBN: 978-1-949523-01-0) and paperback (ISBN : 978-1-949523-00-3).

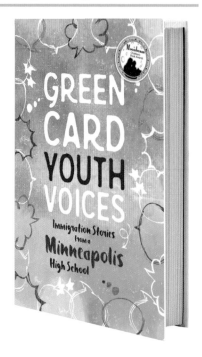

Contents:

- Full color portraits
- 30 personal essays by students from around the world
- Links to digital video stories on the Green Card Voices website
- Foreword by Kao Kalia Yang, award-winning author of *The Latehomecomer* and *The Song Poet*
- Excerpt from *Act4Change: A Green Card Voices Study Guide*
- Glossary

2016 Moonbeam Children's Gold Medal for Multicultural Nonfiction Chapter Book

2016 Foreword INDIES Finalist for Young Adult Nonfiction

2017 Independent Press Awards Winner for Best Young Adult Nonfiction

To purchase online and view a list of retailers, visit greencardvoices.org/books.

Also available on Amazon.

Also Available:
Voices of Immigrant Storytellers:
A Teaching Guide for Middle and High Schools

This ten-lesson curriculum based on the Common Core standards was written and designed by immigrants. The teaching guide progressively unfolds the humanity, diversity, and contributions of new American citizens and situates students' own stories alongside these narratives using eleven Green Card Voices' video narratives. This teaching guide is adaptable for grades 6-12. Available as an ebook (ISBN: 978-0-692-51151-0) and paperback (ISBN : 978-0-692572-81-8).

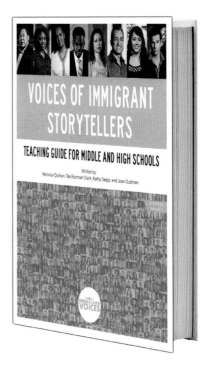

Contents:

- 72 illustrated pages
- 11 Green Card Voices Stories
- 7 ready-to-use worksheets
- 8 classroom activities
- 2 field trip suggestions
- 20 online resources

Available at
greencardvoices.org/books
teacherspayteachers.com
amazon.com

For more information, visit our website at www.greencardvoices.org
or contact us at info@greencardvoices.org